ENGAGE!

A Guide to Involving Your
Consumers in Their Health

ELIZABETH BIERBOWER

Elizabeth Bierbower, Author

John Gettings, Editor

Brad Cain, Executive Editor

Les Masterson, Managing Editor

Matthew Cann, Group Publisher

Karen Stroman, Cover Designer

Mike Mirabello, Senior Graphic Artist

Michael Roberto, Layout Artist

Jean St. Pierre, Director of Operations

Claire Cloutier, Production Manager

Darren Kelly, Books Production Supervisor

Susan Darbyshire, Art Director

Amanda Wilson, Copy Editor

Sada Preisch, Proofreader

Advice given is general. Readers should consult professional counsel for specific legal, ethical, or clinical questions.

Arrangements can be made for quantity discounts. For more information, contact:

HCPro, Inc.
P.O. Box 1168
Marblehead, MA 01945
Telephone: 800/650-6787 or 781/639-1872
Fax: 781/639-2982
E-mail: *customerservice@hcpro.com*

Visit HCPro at its World Wide Web sites:

www.hcpro.com and *www.hcmarketplace.com*

Contents

Contents

About the author

Elizabeth Bierbower

Elizabeth Bierbower is vice president of product innovation for Humana. Beth is responsible for Humana's consumer strategy as well as its product development activities. Most notably, Beth was responsible for the introduction of Humana's SmartSuite product line, the HealthMiles program in partnership with Virgin Life Care, the HumanaAccess card, and is a named inventor on a patent tied to pharmacy-based health reimbursement arrangements.

Beth is a frequent presenter on the topic of consumerism and has authored a number of articles as well as a chapter in the *Managed Care Handbook*. Beth has served as chair of a number of health savings accounts conferences, is a member of the editorial board of Thompson's *Consumer Directed Health Care* newsletter, a member of the AHIP HSA Advisory Council, and has appeared on CNN.

Beth earned a master's degree in public management, graduating with highest honors, from Carnegie Mellon University.

Acknowledgments

I would like to thank the many employers, brokers, consultants, health plan executives, and providers who took the time to share their thoughts on consumer engagement. These conversations helped confirm my beliefs that with commitment and the right approach, we can help consumers engage and take control of their health. I would like to express my gratitude to my colleagues at Humana, who provide an environment that fosters innovation and are dedicated to helping consumers manage their health and benefits every day. Special thanks to the staff at HealthLeaders Media and HCPro for their guidance and patience in this process. Finally, I would like to thank my husband for his encouragement and support in all my endeavors.

Introduction

The debate over whether consumers will engage in managing their health is at an all-time high. The dilemma begins with the question of who is accountable for driving engagement. Should it be solely the employer's responsibility, or should it be left up to the consumer? Is the carrot or the stick the right approach? Should consumers be rewarded for simply being engaged in their healthcare or only for outcomes that demonstrate good health? As with any issue, multiple views exist.

The cynics' view

Cynics tell us not to waste our money rewarding, cajoling, or even coercing consumers to better health. They believe that the effort is a waste of capital and human resources that can and should be better spent elsewhere. These cynics speak from experience when they tell us consumers will not participate in a program just because their employer or doctor asks (or tells) them to do so. The cynics have tried wellness programs and used carrots and sticks to get consumers to lose weight or lower their blood pressure and have not seen the kind of results that merit the effort. Cigarette packaging tells consumers that smoking has dangerous consequences, yet smokers continue to light up. Consumers have been given every chance to change, yet we see that most consumers ignore the signs, pleas, and even mandates and live as if today's actions won't affect tomorrow. Our attempts to engage consumers have resulted in low participation rates and virtually nonexistent return on investment. And despite great efforts, healthcare costs have continued to climb year after year.

Maybe the cynics are right. If the current approaches were even moderately effective, millions of adults wouldn't be smoking and obesity wouldn't be a top concern on the national healthcare agenda. The prevalence of chronic conditions and comorbid disease states would be dramatically diminished if consumers were engaged in their health and healthcare costs themselves were not increasing at double the inflation rate. The cynics do have a point. The view across the horizon looks pretty gloomy. Does this mean we should throw our arms up and let the chips fall where they may?

Challenging the cynics

On the other side of the debate, a new group of consumer health activists have emerged, although many will tell you have they have been championing the cause all along. These health activists come in all shapes and sizes, with different titles and incomes and have varying views of what works and what doesn't. These activists are brokers, employers, consultants, healthcare providers, and even health plans. Employer-based health activists can be found throughout the company environment, from the executive office to the human resources department to the frontline worker. Other health activists work from the outside in and serve as engagement champions with their clients, working to create customized programs or arrangements designed to fill critical gaps. Their enthusiasm is contagious and their numbers are growing. These individuals challenge the cynics and tell us that consumers will become engaged if we as employers, brokers, providers, and consultants do a better job of encouraging and enticing them to come into the fold. Health activists take a comprehensive approach to engagement and encourage more, not less, interaction.

Undeterred, even by past failures, health activists are piloting and testing their methods to see what works in getting consumers to engage in their health. These individuals develop low-cost, tactical approaches designed to meet the needs of their consumer population. They don't let convention get in their way and their ideas are derived from identifying and filling gaps, often using unconventional thinking. Health activists are not following a predetermined path. Rather, they are constantly reviewing health and productivity costs, assessing their environment and the needs of their employees, clients, or patients to determine what methods they can improve and add to better the health of their population. Lack of funding or human resources is generally viewed as an opportunity and not a barrier. These activists find low-cost approaches to engage consumers, often flying under the radar screen of the finance executives. These champions are making incremental changes that collectively have a significant effect.

Make no mistake, health activists, such as employers, brokers, and consultants, are not exclusively focused on engagement because it is the right thing to do. They also see the financial benefit to consumer engagement and view it as a critical component to mitigating rising healthcare trends in the short and long term. Healthcare providers know that engaging their consumers can result not only in improved compliance and health outcomes, but also in patient retention.

    Engage! A Guide to Involving Your Consumers in Their Health

Which enrollment approach is the best?

The debate moves beyond the question of whether consumers can be engaged in their health to which approach is best—an employer- or consumer-based approach? "There are two competing philosophies," according to Celia Huber, Partner in McKinsey & Company's healthcare consulting practice based in Pittsburgh, PA. "One view places the responsibility squarely on the shoulders of the consumer while the other approach puts the employer in the driver's seat."

Consumer-based approach

Many health plans have taken the consumer-based approach by designing products, programs, and services to connect with members at all levels of health. They believe the direct-to-consumer approach is the best means to get the individual to step up and be accountable for his or her health by ensuring that the individual has financial incentives and the support tools and programs to make appropriate decisions. The consumer driven health plan, or CDHP, was the initial tactic taken by health plans to spur the consumer to action. More recently, health plans and administrators have shifted to a broader view of consumerism and consumer engagement that moves beyond the plan design. Health plans recognize that while financial incentives certainly get the consumer's attention, they need to offer the consumer additional support programs and services that help create an environment for engagement. Without the additional consumerism components, cost-shifting, rather than consumer engagement, occurs. The consumer approach doesn't eliminate the role of the employer; it shifts the employer from a paternalistic position to one of a facilitator, allowing direct and ongoing access to employees and dependents.

Employer-based approach

The employer-based approach is prevalent in the market and places the employer in the middle of the action, using the worksite as the "hub" for creating and driving behavior change. In this approach, the employer assumes the responsibility of identifying, purchasing, and/or developing and implementing programs, directly or through use of health plans and other third parties. The employer decides which programs provide value for its consumers and which ones will be offered. The level of integration among the various healthcare partners is dictated by the employer, thereby driving the end consumer experience. Program integration is an important concept that is explored later on and can have a significant impact on program success. The majority of employers, brokers, consultants, and healthcare providers view the employer-based model as the approach best positioned for success. Establishing a captive environment in which a consumer receives information from a party for whom he or she has some level of trust appears to be the right strategy to achieve a culture of wellness.

Regardless of the model you prefer, moving toward a culture of health and engagement is a journey that requires a long-term vision and commitment. Like any journey, it will take time and it will often be challenging to see what lies ahead. You will need to consider the following questions: What will the organization look like, and how will your consumers act if a culture of engagement is achieved?

The "Velcro hug"

The picture of the future will vary from organization to organization as each entity will embrace and manifest engagement in different ways. However, an unusual image may serve as a good visual representation of what it means for a consumer to engage with his or her health activist, whether it's the employer, provider, or health plan: Picture the consumer wrapped in a pair of Velcro arms. Jonathan Lord, MD, chief innovation officer, Humana, created this image of a consumer wrapped in a "Velcro hug." It symbolizes Humana's philosophy: reach out to consumers, provide motivation for them to engage in, and continue to demonstrate healthy behaviors. Most important, however, is to provide support to the consumer through every stage of engagement, never letting him or her slip from the providers' grasp, retaining a firm grip on the consumer to ensure that he or she can sustain a healthy lifestyle over the long term. The image of a Velcro hug conveys the desire to create a level of stickiness between the consumer and the employer or provider that results in an ongoing relationship.

Embarking on a journey to change the individuals in your organization from passive, uninvolved individuals to savvy, engaged consumers requires the following:

+ A commitment by you and the leaders (formal or informal) in your organization to create a culture of engagement and health over time;

+ A plan that maps your journey over a period of years, detailing activities, programs, services, and educational efforts that will be deployed to engage your consumers;

+ Measurement of your program outcomes, including successes and failures, as well impacts on healthcare, productivity costs, and the organization's morale; and

* Perseverance to continue when some initiatives fail or the organization's commitment to a culture of engagement begins to waiver.

This guide is designed to get you started by giving you a framework that includes some concepts and ideas to drive a culture of health and healthy behaviors within your organization. As you read on, you will understand the components of a successful consumer engagement strategy and how to implement these pieces to create a program that works for your consumers, your clients, and even your patients. Throughout this guide, we'll share examples and stories of what others are doing to reach out and wrap their consumers in Velcro hugs.

Throughout this guide you will find practical examples of programs and tactics you can deploy in your organization. Use it as a starting point to design your own program, one that incorporates the beliefs and values of your organization and fits your consumer population. You should start by taking an idea and improving upon it or tailoring an approach: Customization is important to ensure adoption and success.

So sit back, grab a healthy snack, and learn how you can begin to develop a plan for wrapping your consumers in a Velcro hug, ultimately driving your organization to a culture of health and engagement.

CHAPTER 1

A view from the top
Strategies for securing leadership buy-in, funding, and a commitment to culture change

> *"Culture is not made up but something that evolves which is human."*
>
> – Edward T. Hall, renowned anthropologist

Organizations that have implemented successful health engagement strategies typically share a common trait: They have created a culture around health, wellness, and personal accountability (this will be referred to as a "culture of health"). Creating a culture of health helps set employee and senior management expectations and lays the foundation for sustainability. Incorporating health into your culture makes a statement that health engagement is part of your company's DNA; it is who you are and how you do business. Including health as a cultural component also demonstrates the commitment you have to your consumers and shows them that health is important. "The desire to change must permeate your whole culture," says Jed Skeete, executive vice president of McGriff, Seibels and Williams, a brokerage and consulting firm specializing in Fortune 100 companies. While a culture is intangible, there are a few simple components that can help your organization achieve such a

culture: a champion(s), commitment, and health infusion. Let's explore each of these cultural aspects in further detail.

Identify a senior champion(s)

The champion is an individual or number of individuals that are committed to engaging employees and helping them improve their health. Some may initially think that champions can only originate from the senior management team and must be the CEO. If you can get your top officer or a member of your senior team to be a champion then do it. The more prominent the individual is within the organization, the more likely your consumers will stop and listen to what he or she has to say. However, champions can come from many areas within the organization. Your champions may be employees who are viewed as influencers within the organization, a respected supervisor or manager, or perhaps someone from human resources.

The perception of this individual and his or her scope of influence is what matters and is more important than title or position.

Credibility plays a big role in changing your organization's culture, and the more credibility you can gain by having a senior champion, the better. Former Arkansas Governor Mike Huckabee is a good example of a champion. Not only was Huckabee's goal better health for the state's workers, he wanted to control the state's rising healthcare costs. As governor, he was a very visible figure to the state's employees and the perfect person to effectively drive health throughout the organization. He made it his mission to talk with employees about improving their health and helped propel health and lifestyle issues to the national agenda.

Management must play a key role in setting the "health strategy" and then delivering the message throughout the organization at every opportunity. Other top "C" leaders such as the chief operating officer (COO) or chief financial officer (CFO) may serve in the role of the champion. However, you should avoid asking the chief human resources officer to serve in the role of key health champion. This individual should be a champion, but not the lead champion. This is to avoid the possibility of your consumers confusing a cultural change with a human resources initiative. In other words, creating a culture of health is not one aspect of your business—it is business.

A change at the top?

Some CEOs or senior team members may be opposed to any activities that lend themselves to engaging consumers in their health. This makes the health activist's job more difficult. One human resources director shared that the culture shift toward wellness began with a change in CEOs. The prior CEO did not see value in initiatives to drive healthy behaviors and as a result, almost every initiative was dismissed. The new CEO embraced health initiatives and served as the company champion, bringing rapid and positive changes to the company culture. Given the continuing rise in health-care costs, it's unlikely that CEOs and senior management will take a stance against improving the health of their consumers.

Even if the management team is "neutral" at best and, more realistically, not on board at all with the idea of engagement, keep in mind that commitment comes in many different forms. Although the ideal is to have your CEO championing the program, you'll find you can still move forward and make great strides without the overt support of your senior team. "As long as you have permission to move forward and try new ideas, you can still be successful," states Celia Huber of McKinsey & Company. "Simply not being deterred from implementing wellness or incentives and rewards programs or offering health plans designed to encourage healthy behaviors provides a sufficient foundation to move forward and show initial results by creating a platform for consumer engagement." This "environment of permission" is prevalent within many organizations. Health activists see this lack of commitment from the senior team as an opportunity to move forward with their ideas and slowly ingrain healthy behaviors and attitudes into the culture. The permissive approach may take a little longer, but with time and some positive results, may lead to a commitment from the senior team.

Build momentum through middle management

Expand your champions beyond the senior team. While it's certainly important to have senior leadership buy-in and support, champions can come from many areas of the organization: the top, bottom, or somewhere in between. One of the management groups that is the slowest to embrace a culture of health is middle management, e.g., line supervisors and managers. "If your middle managers are not on board, you will have issues," says Sarah Novak, director, benefits, Plexus Corp in Neenah, WI, an international electronics manufacturer. "We had to prove to the supervisors that these programs were of value." Barb Thode, human resources manager, Orion Corporation in Grafton, WI, concurs: "Frontline supervisors

can be a bit of a challenge, and gaining their buy-in is important to gaining and sustaining momentum for a cultural shift."

Middle managers operate in a world where maintaining current processes and procedures is critical to delivering a high-quality product or service on time. They fear that the introduction of new, unknown elements into the workday can result in disruption of their routines. Ultimately, many worry that the introduction of healthy activities will hurt productivity and reflect poorly on their team's overall performance. They may be right. The idea of a workplace-based approach is to engage the employee when you have him or her captive for eight to nine hours a day. You cannot expect your consumers to give up their break and lunch times for every initiative. This means the middle manager's fear will likely come true—the employee will have to step away from his or her daily work routine in order to participate.

Address these concerns head-on by soliciting the input of your middle managers, and in particular, get their feedback on the timing of your activities. The middle management team can help you arrange times and perhaps even design activities that will have minimal negative impact on productivity during the initial rollout. When these middle managers give you input, they will also take pride in the role they played to introduce the program.

Recruit the real influencers

Choosing to include employees from the beginning is generally a good idea, but it's important that you get the right people. In most companies, an undercurrent drives the culture, regardless of what the senior management team or the company mission statement says. This undercurrent or invisible force includes a number of individuals who may not be in official positions of leadership but still wield a substantial amount of influence with your consumers. These individuals may be sought out by others looking for advice and counsel on the inner workings of your organization and may be viewed as authority figures. Their words and actions (and at times inaction) are closely followed by and carry weight with your consumers. Organizations that want pervasive, sustainable change may look to engage these individuals in the development and implementation of their strategy.

Prior to identifying the right people to drive change, begin by defining the role these consumers will play.

- Will these individuals have input without authority?

- Will they have a voice directly with and present to senior management?

- Will they serve as ambassadors and talk with others inside the organization about the strategy and the reasons certain decisions were made?

"Typically these individuals are asked to serve in an advisory capacity rather than in a governing or steering committee role," states Jay Savan, principal, Towers Perrin, a global human resources and financial services advisory firm. "These employees represent the view of the customer and agree to be educated on your strategy and approach to employee health." Create a description that individuals can review as part of their consideration for the role. Putting the role parameters in writing will help your volunteers understand where their input begins and ends. Also, let them know the authority level of the team in general. If senior management has the option to override recommendations and decisions of the team, let them know this in advance.

It is important to carefully select which individuals will participate on the advisory team. Placing the wrong people in an advisory capacity can undermine your strategy. For example, selecting an individual to participate on the advisory team because he or she is known to be vocal might seem like a good idea. However, if the person is not well respected by fellow employees, or can't work well in a team environment, his or her participation can be a hindrance to achieving the desired objectives. Selecting the appropriate individuals is so essential to supporting its strategy that Towers Perrin has developed a proprietary methodology to help organizations get the right mix of personalities and attributes to create an effective advisory team. "Choosing the right people helps the employer get at the underlying trust issue that is often at risk when change occurs. By involving employees who can validate to their peers how decisions were vetted and made, you gain a level of trust and confidence with your employee population," says Savan.

Convert commitment into funding

Gaining commitment to the concept of building a culture of health is the first step. Senior management is on board and internal champions have been identified. The time has come to receive commitment to obtain both the human and financial resources required to build the infrastructure to support your consumers in developing and demonstrating healthy behaviors.

One organization may want to build an on-site fitness center to make it convenient for individuals to fit exercise into their daily routine. Others may want to provide health screenings or fund wellness and health savings accounts as a means of rewarding individuals for engaging in healthy behaviors or maintaining healthy

outcomes. All of these initiatives require a budget. Management must now make the monetary commitment to produce a benefit in the future. You should take into consideration the possibility that the impact on healthcare costs may not be immediately evident.

Show me the money

For some, the lack of a solid financial return may require a leap of faith—or will it? Is it really necessary to create a cost-benefit analysis to understand that helping individuals to stop smoking will reduce healthcare costs, or that being within the right weight range can reduce the risk of heart attack or decrease comorbidities? The answer may be yes.

In most companies, we have to sharpen the pencils and demonstrate that an initiative or program will result in savings. Fifteen years ago, Barbara Day was providing wellness programs to major corporations located in the greater Louisville, KY, area. "The desire for these programs began to slow because we could not collect the data to provide a definitive return on investment (ROI). Employers wanted to know they were getting their money's worth," says Day, now the owner and publisher of two health magazines serving Kentucky and Indiana.

If proof of ROI is required, put your broker or health plan representative to work. Many studies exist on the benefits of providing wellness, chronic-condition, and other programs; companies that offer these programs have this data readily available. Keep the analysis simple and relevant. The programs you offer should be categorized by serious health conditions and should focus on keeping healthy consumers healthy. Limited funding may steer you to address only one high utilization area first, so choose your tactic based on solid data.

If, for instance, your claims data show that your largest issue is related to work site injuries, then your first initiative should focus on workplace safety. Prioritize the remaining initiatives based on potential cost savings to a point, but don't overlook activities that may appear to have low return or may not even be tied to a solid return. It's important to offer programs that appeal to those that are moderately or very healthy and to encourage and support them in maintaining their health.

Be penny-wise: Shop for value

While many health activists are concerned over the lack of adequate funding to cover the cost of all the desired initiatives, it's common to see that in the quest to provide best-in-class services, some organizations pay for services they could be receiving for free. This drive for perfection may be detracting from the ability to fund more healthy activities. If you are in a position of overseeing the dollars spent on consumer engagement initiatives, ensure that your team is truly getting the best value and not paying more for what may be incremental and nonvalue-added services or features. The opportunity to minimize costs may be right in front of you. Look to your broker, health plan, or third-party administrator for programs or services. Health insurers, for example, typically provide disease management, wellness, and sometimes rewards programs free of charge to employers who are fully insured.

The health insurer is at risk for claims, so it makes good business sense to include these services, which have the potential to improve health, in the cost of the premium. In addition, your carrier will usually do a good job of integrating the data collected as part of a wellness program into its information management systems. This integration helps to ensure that individuals in need are referred to clinical programs, such as disease management. Before you reach for your checkbook to pay for a program, determine if your plan administrator can provide you with a viable solution that is either free or less expensive. Since your health plan also holds your claims data, ask them whether they can perform an analysis on the impact of your initiatives. If you are using the health insurer's programs and services, volunteer to be used as a case study that they can share with other prospective and existing clients. You get the analysis and program support you need and the health insurer gets to tell your story. This is a win-win situation for both parties. To learn about other ways your health plan may be able to help you reach your engagement goals, refer to Chapter 11.

Engage! A Guide to Involving Your Consumers in Their Health

Gain personal commitments

Once you have secured the monetary commitment of your senior team to fund your health improvement initiatives, get their personal commitment. Employees are more likely to engage and stay active in a program if they know the top leaders are personally buying in. Personal commitment by the president, CEO, or owner sends a strong message to your employees that you are serious about change. When a CEO shows employees that she wears a pedometer each day to track her steps or that he "knows his numbers" (associated with blood pressure or cholesterol), it tells employees that the individual has made a personal commitment. Former Governor Huckabee is an example of a leader that demonstrated personal commitment. Huckabee used to shy away from healthcare-related issues when he was carrying an extra 100+ pounds. He undertook a personal transformation and used his own experience to help drive a culture of health in the state of Arkansas, serving as an inspiration to many. People like to know that their leaders are just like them and that they struggle with the same bad habits and health issues. Sending the message that your management team members are personally committed and trying to change their own healthy behaviors will come across loud and clear. Encourage your management team to wear pedometers and attend the on-site health fairs (remember, actions speak louder than words.) The School Board of Broward County, FL, knows the meaning of commitment from the top. Members of its board of directors were participants in one of the "healthy heart" team competitions. The healthy heart competition is a pedometer-based walking program that includes a six-week competition among the various departments in the school district. This is a great example of actions speaking louder than words.

Commit to a healthy culture change

Many organizations find it challenging to describe their existing culture, let alone create a culture with health as a cornerstone. Successful companies, however, make health a priority in everything they do, and this becomes embedded in the company culture. Every action is carefully examined to determine whether it aligns with the company's healthy values. Organizations that want culture change ensure healthy selections are predominant in the vending machines and cafeteria or build an on-site fitness club with extended hours and offer a variety of classes to ensure the broadest appeal and access to its consumers. They may also unlock the doors to encourage use of the stairs and provide the time at work for individuals to learn about and develop healthy lifestyles.

Committed managers talk about the company's health at every venue from staff and budget meetings to leadership development programs.

They talk about it with all employees from the corporate office, from the manufacturing floor to the field. Families are also included in the mix since they are the support system (or not) for your consumers after their work is done. With continuous and consistent messaging, your consumers will soon understand that this drive for health engagement is not simply another fad.

Conclusion

You'll learn more about how others have developed or are driving toward a culture of health as you read on, but let's take a minute to think about the journey ahead. Building a healthy culture takes time, period. Moreover, consumer engagement is not a program, or a service or a campaign; it's a journey. This journey is about encouraging your consumers to adopt better habits that will produce positive effects on their health, work, family, and lives.

Journeys take time and do not always have definitive endings. In fact, most journeys include exploring new paths and territories that were not on the original plan, and this mindset should be embraced by the management team from the outset. Setting a one-, two-, or three-year plan with the intention of folding if the objectives aren't met sets your organization up for failure. Think of this journey as a long-term investment (day traders should stop reading right now!) and as with most investments, paybacks may not always be evident in the short term. When you ask for a commitment from your senior team, help them understand that the process is a journey and that they need to continue to support these initiatives, even when the peaks quickly turn into valleys. Show them the plan, let them know there will be detours along the way (and maybe an accident or two). But let them know that with the right amount of fuel (money, please!) and perseverance you will make progress, and the journey will have a positive effect on the health and attitudes of your consumers, your organization's culture, and the bottom line. Buckle up, grab your Velcro, and let's examine some real-life examples and tactics you can deploy as you begin your journey.

CHAPTER  2

The power of numbers
Practical ways to explain the cost-of-healthcare dilemma to your consumers

> *"America enjoys the best health care in the world, but the best is no good if folks can't afford it, access it and doctors can't provide it."*
>
> – Bill Frist, physician and former Republican senator from Tennessee

Each year, consumers see their share of healthcare costs rise. Their premium contributions are increased, copays are raised, and high deductibles are introduced in the form of consumer-driven health plans. When consumers look at their paychecks, they simply don't get it. Increased healthcare costs have eaten away at their annual pay raise, lowering their standard of living each year.

Small employers in particular are struggling to offer health benefits, with some dropping coverage and forcing consumers into the individual insurance or uninsured pool. Many organizations subsidize only the employee premium, causing some consumers to look elsewhere, including Medicaid and children's programs to cover their family members. Large employers are also affected by the healthcare-cost dilemma. Healthcare costs are burdening already lean profit margins, putting pressure on

management to outsource jobs and reduce benefits. Healthcare providers are also feeling the pressure. Reimbursement rates are not automatically linked to inflation. To maintain the prior year's earnings, providers may have to handle a heavier patient load. Consumers, employers, and providers are inextricably linked in the healthcare-cost equation. When costs spin out of control, all parties lose.

Following the doctor's orders

Increasingly, consumers are feeling helpless and confused. They believe they're following the rules that employers and health plans have set over the years. For example, many consumers use the health plan's network providers and dutifully pay their copays each time they visit the doctor or get a prescription. How then can they be responsible for rising healthcare costs?

Individuals struggle with the idea of consumerism in healthcare. Why do they need to shop around when a doctor tells them what they need and where they should receive the care? With the exception of routine diagnostic tests like mammograms, consumers don't order tests themselves; the doctors order the tests. The doctor wouldn't order a test that isn't needed; the doctor always knows best, right? Consumers aren't really asking for these tests, are they? Isn't it the health plan's job to get the best deal with the healthcare providers? "Isn't that why I am paying these premiums?" consumers ask.

Your consumers may, in fact, be requesting unnecessary tests and services. Where they decide to receive care can have a significant impact on price. Whether your consumers are patients, employees, or health plan members, it is your responsibility to help them understand their role in driving utilization, provider rates, and overall costs. Let's explore what you can do to help your consumers understand the effects that rising healthcare costs have on them, personally and professionally.

Begin with a conversation about context

The topic of education will be addressed more closely in Chapter 3, and specific examples will be provided throughout this guide. But to give consumers a complete view of their role, we must first set the context for rising healthcare costs; this starts with a conversation. Engagement will not happen unless you promote transparency by having a two-way, open dialogue with your consumers. What does transparency mean? It means that you're sharing all of the appropriate information with consumers, good news and bad. Transparency also means you'll share information on a consistent basis and not limit healthcare meetings to times when a crisis exists.

Lack of consistency will hurt your credibility with consumers. When push comes to shove and you need employees and patients rallying around to help control costs, you won't get their support without consistency. Consumers are smart. While they may not understand everything you share, they do understand the organization's level of commitment. Read on to see what kind of information is useful in setting the context.

Know your numbers

The first conversation should be about the numbers. You should share with employees how much your company spends on healthcare costs as well as how much employees spend on average out-of-pocket healthcare costs. (Hitting the wallet is sure to grab their attention!) While you may get a glazed look from some, others will be astounded at the amount spent annually on healthcare. Even those that were not on board at first will gradually begin to understand your message.

Put the numbers into context by using other business figures that your consumers know and understand. For example, if your employees understand earnings-per-share, define the impact healthcare expenditures have on this indicator as well as other bottom line profit measures. The auto makers have done a good job of sharing the effect that healthcare costs have on the price of a car with not only their employees and the unions but also with health plans, providers, politicians, and consumers in general. Another good way to put the numbers in context is to tie in productivity indicators. For instance, the school board of Broward County, FL, has done its homework and knows that shaving off one sick day per employee, per year will result in a million dollars in savings. That's knowing your numbers!

Demonstrate to consumers the trade-offs your organization makes because of rising healthcare costs. If every 1% increase in healthcare costs results in a decrease in the research and development or information technology budget, let your employees know it. If healthcare costs are prohibiting the company from expanding into new markets, help them understand why. The measure with which most people will relate is the annual wage or salary increase. Translate

the effect that healthcare cost increases have on raises and the light bulb will soon click on.

Also, knowing what your competitors spend on healthcare can be very powerful. Most employees want their organizations to succeed, and knowing that the competition has an edge on healthcare costs provides significant motivation to take action. Use simple, colorful graphs and charts when displaying the numbers. Don't be afraid to have fun with this information. Although this is a very important topic, it may be more readily understood and retained if it's presented in an interesting way. Any approach that engages your consumers and helps them understand what really drives healthcare costs is probably acceptable.

Setting the context is not a one-time initiative. To ensure that your consumers fully comprehend the effects that escalating healthcare costs have on your business, choose the indicators that are important to you and your consumers and then tell your consumers. Once these indicators are identified, tell your consumers again and again how the company is performing against them. For example, if the increase in healthcare expenditures added two cents to earnings-per-share or translated to 20% of your total budget, tell consumers the new numbers each year in the same terms. Publishing consistent context and setting indicators each year helps consumers to understand where the organization was the year before—or even five years before—and where it is today. It's essential that they know first, at a high level, whether the healthcare-cost situation has improved or whether they have an even bigger problem. Your consumers can only make these comparisons when the benchmarks remain consistent.

Dig deeper into the numbers

Now that you've gotten your consumers' attention with some very large numbers, educate them about the forces driving those numbers. We all know that new technologies, new drugs, and increased use of services are major factors in costs; however, you need to know your numbers. Generalities are meaningless. You must share with individuals in your organization the trends in your population at-large and, if possible, in each of your office or plant locations. If you're a small company, you may not have access to the detailed data, but you can still ensure that your consumers understand what's driving costs in your risk pool.

Where do you turn for help? Talk with your broker and health plan representative to determine what exactly drives healthcare costs. Catastrophic events can always create one-time price spikes; however, if you peel back the onion, you'll see that the majority of your healthcare expense is related to utilization (or

in some cases, lack of utilization of services) or specific conditions. For example, you may find that 20% of your workers have chronic conditions that are driving 70–80% of the costs. Perhaps medication compliance is a problem, resulting in more hospitalizations or use of the emergency room. On the other hand, excessive utilization of brand-name drugs may be driving high prescription drug costs.

Location-specific data is important to determine if you have a network access issue or if a particular provider is driving higher utilization. Don't stop by looking at high utilization, look for underuse of services as well. For example, you may find low participation in your health plan's clinical programs, which means that individuals with chronic conditions may not be accessing the right care or may not be getting the care they need. Remember to always look at both sides of the equation, high and low utilization, when determining driving forces behind increasing costs, as both can have significant effect.

Set realistic goals

After establishing the baseline activity, set goals for the upcoming year. If the baseline assessment shows that only 10% of individuals currently participate in the health plan's clinical programs, then set a goal to increase participation for the next year. Depending on your company culture, you may want to ask your consumers for their input in determining goals. When individuals are involved in creating goals, they will be more motivated to meet them. Publish and discuss your goals on a regular basis. Limiting the dissemination of this information to once per year will do little to motivate consumers to change behavior. Goals should be reviewed at key management and employee meetings. Additionally, interim and annual results should be posted in places where individuals congregate, e.g., the lunch room and vending machines. When you know you are not meeting specific goals, ramp up the communications to get your message out. Individuals like to know they're making a difference, and sharing the information with them time and again will help keep the issue at the front of their minds.

Providers: Go public with your numbers

Providers have multiple roles in healthcare: They render services, are employers and employees, and, most certainly, are healthcare consumers. Therefore, share with your employees what's driving your healthcare costs, but also understand and share what's happening within your own practice or hospital. How are you performing as a healthcare provider? How do you compare against your competition or the national average? As a healthcare provider your employees should also know the numbers around your performance at large. By sharing this information, you help employees understand your contribution to improving efficiency in the health system. More important, as your employees become more educated, they will in turn help educate your consumers.

Consider sharing information with a broader audience. Performance information can be shared with consumers in your community to demonstrate your level of competence. In some states, such as Pennsylvania, hospitals are required to provide data on hospital admissions. Providers often view these efforts with a wary eye and cite bad data, or the fact that they have patients with higher severity scores, as a reason to ignore the data. Healthcare providers may fear that sharing information reveals they are not the best in a specific category or service will cause some consumers to seek care elsewhere. Healthcare providers should consider embracing the concept of publishing performance data. For many, sharing data can create a competitive advantage. For example, providers can tout the services in which they excel.

But what should you do if your data doesn't look all that good? You have to determine whether you're committed to transparency. Begin by sharing information in one area. Perhaps you're known as a high-quality provider of cardiac care. Publish information about this service, including areas that need improvement and what you are doing to improve. Perhaps you have upgraded equipment or brought in a new cardiothoracic surgeon to improve outcomes. Sharing this information will give consumers the confidence that you are committed to providing the highest quality of care.

Health plans, also take note. We share positive information front and center on our Web sites, such as whether or not we have achieved a form of accreditation or if we scored well on a satisfaction survey. We don't, however, typically reveal our weaknesses and what we are doing to overcome them. Consider taking a bold approach. Grade yourself as a health plan and then let consumers know what you are going to do to improve performance. (Refer to the section on targeted messaging in Chapter 3 to direct your message to interested consumers.) Consumers might feel better about taking a chance on selecting your health plan again next year if they know you've just made a significant investment in your clinical programs or a change to get their claims paid faster.

Balancing information with privacy
You've identified the healthcare cost drivers within your specific population (employees, patients, or health plan members), but how do you share this information in a meaningful way and ensure you are maintaining privacy? Frame your findings to ensure you're not sharing

employee-specific information. A very large employer with thousands of employees may feel comfortable stating that 20% of employees are diabetics while a small employer may talk more generally about chronic conditions. Slicing data by gender or age may enable you to get to the level of granularity needed to make the point without breaching privacy.

For example, sharing that only 70% of eligible women are getting routine mammograms as a part of their preventive care would, for most organizations, be an appropriate level of information. Regardless of the size of your company, you can find a way to provide an appropriate level of information.

Focus on a few drivers
Focus on the top three to five drivers of your healthcare costs. If it is your first attempt at sharing information, you may want to stick with three for the first year or two. Presenting too much information may result in losing your audience. Services that impact the majority of your consumers should be addressed first.

For example, it's easy to talk about prescription drugs because the majority of individuals, including those that are healthy, will have experience with these services. Compare your organization's use of generics in relation to industry standards and your competitors. If your health plan participants are not taking advantage of lower-cost brands and generics, identify the problematic drugs; share the costs, the alternatives, and where consumers can get the best deal. Also, list the potential savings to the consumer and the organization. Including the organization's savings demonstrates your commitment to transparency. If you do not present the full view, consumers will think you have something to hide.

Earlier, we emphasized the need for consistency from year to year with indicators. This holds true for those key business indicators (e.g., earnings-per-share) and the large numbers around healthcare expenditures.

However, as you move forward each year, there may be a need to add a new indicator. For example, introduction of a high-deductible health plan with a health savings account may lead to tracking the amounts of enrollee contributions. As long as the indicators are highly relevant to your consumers and you have good continuity year after year, it is not only permissible but desirable to introduce new (and, in some cases, retire) indicators.

International considerations

When we think about healthcare costs we're typically focused on our employees in the United States. Do you need to worry about healthcare costs if you have international locations? Yes! Employers that manage international locations are seeing the cost of care in other countries beginning to catch up with the United States.

Even in countries with national healthcare systems, employers may be required to offer supplemental coverage policies that provide access to private facilities or cover services not provided under the national system. Plexus Corp has begun to introduce some of the techniques deployed in the United States to its locations in other parts of the world. Remember that while healthcare may be delivered locally, the cost dilemma extends beyond U.S. borders.

Communicate, communicate, communicate

Once you have set the context, determined what is driving your healthcare costs, and have agreed upon your goals, the next step is simple (at least in theory). Get this information in front of your consumers at every possible interaction. Sometimes this means pushing the information out or pulling consumers in. Chapter 3 gives you very specific examples of communications channels, so we will limit this discussion to a simple phrase: Try anything. Don't rely on consumers to visit your Web sites to gather information. Consumers are generally too busy to scour the Internet or intranet to determine whether they might save a few bucks. Use traditional and nontraditional methods to get your message heard.

Help consumers understand they have a role

Even after understanding healthcare cost drivers, such as chronic conditions or use of brand-name drugs, consumers may still be at a loss as to what they can do to make a meaningful difference. Many consumers may have the same attitude toward impacting healthcare costs as they do toward impacting an election (their vote won't make a difference). If asked, some consumers might respond that they have no role in driving healthcare costs.

"Employees don't understand they have a role to play in healthcare. They believe their responsibility ends when they hand the identification card over to the provider. You can't engage individuals until they understand they have a role in managing their own healthcare," says Dianne Kiehl, executive director, Business

Healthcare Group (BHCG) of Southeast Wisconsin. Engaging your consumers in the healthcare-cost dilemma requires them to understand the impact they have as individuals on healthcare costs.

Provide your consumers with real-life examples of how they can play a role in curbing rising healthcare costs. Begin by creating a dialogue that will get them thinking about whether they're active or passive healthcare consumers. The following questions will help get the conversation rolling:

- Do you feel you don't get your money's worth from your doctor visit if you leave without a prescription or a referral for a test?

- Do you ask your healthcare provider if there are lower-cost alternatives when he or she suggests a diagnostic test such as an MRI?

- Did you ask for a generic equivalent when you filled your last prescription?

- Do you use mail-order pharmacy for maintenance medications?

- Did you shop for the lowest-cost mammogram in your area?

     Engage! A Guide to Involving Your Consumers in Their Health

♦ Did you get a flu shot for free at work or a community event, or did you go to your doctor and pay a copay?

If you are just beginning to engage your consumers (or feel they need a refresher), ask these questions and see the reaction you get. Certainly some consumer responses will demonstrate that you have some shoppers within your organization. Others might wonder why these questions are being asked. They might be wondering whether costs are going up again or more rules have been introduced. Be frank with your consumers about why you're initiating this dialogue. The reason is simple enough: You want to gauge where your population is on the scale of consumerism.

If you're a healthcare provider, you too should be asking your employees and patients these questions. Help set patient expectations before the exam. Imagine patients being satisfied that they had a good visit with their doctor even though they left without a prescription. Patients trust their doctors even more than their employers and certainly more than their health plans. Take advantage of this opportunity. Make one of the goals of your practice or hospital be having the most educated patients. The more your patients are educated about their role in healthcare costs, the more likely they are to be satisfied with you and your services.

Provide more information

One way to help individuals understand their role is to share information about the costs of care and the impact those costs have on them personally and professionally. Despite efforts, providers, employers and health plans alike have not done a good job of helping consumers understand the cost dilemma. In fact, many health insurance benefit features such as copays have masked the true cost of healthcare. For the cost of a copay, a consumer can get office visit services ranging from $100 to $200 or more. What a great deal! Yet consumers complain when the copay is increased by $5 because they have no idea of the actual value provided to them by their health insurance. Post the costs of office visits for routine services, as well as the top 20 brand-name drugs (based on use by your consumers.) Next to these costs, post the cost of alternative services, e.g., calling the nurse advice line or using a convenient care clinic. Include the generic equivalent options for the medications and let them know which local pharmacies offer the best deals (remember to factor in your health plan's discount).

Let consumers know that their decisions can have an immediate impact on their individual healthcare costs, as well of those of the organization. These are all decisions that are typically within the full control of the consumer. You may think that consumers already know they have control over these choices, but many do not. Some patients would not think to ask for a generic medication for fear that they would receive a less effective drug or alienate their doctor. Others may not understand that, even when you have health insurance, the cost of one specific drug can vary by pharmacy location. This information is particularly important for individuals enrolled in a high-deductible, consumer-driven health plan, as they are typically responsible for a large share of the pharmacy costs until the deductible is satisfied.

In addition to cost information, you'll need to focus on the impact that certain lifestyles have on healthcare costs. Present large numbers that will grab your consumers' attention.

For example, you may be able to share what the additional annual and lifetime healthcare costs are for individuals that smoke or have a body mass index (BMI) above the recommended range. Include the impact on the consumer's wallet as well. Once an individual understands that his or her lifestyle might cost him or her an additional $50,000 in healthcare costs over a lifetime, he may just reconsider reaching for that donut. "Involving employees in their health is the only way we can begin to reduce costs.

The majority of health conditions are directly related to lifestyles," says Barb Thode of Orion Corporation. Gather all the data you can on the impacts of lifestyle and communicate, communicate, communicate.

Celebrate good times

Celebrate as many successes as you reasonably can, including individual and team successes. Achieving key milestones as a group should be noted at meetings and through other channels used to infuse health throughout your culture. Showcase these triumphs. Make them a big deal! Be specific in sharing with individuals exactly how their efforts have contributed to the progress.

For example, if large claims have decreased or moderated around certain conditions because more individuals have joined disease management programs, let your consumers know they have had an impact. One employer shared with its employees the direct impact they had on healthcare costs, including what plan participants saved by using tax-advantaged accounts and shifting to new plan designs. While you need to be sensitive to individual privacy, many consumers enjoy and thrive on the recognition they receive for achieving a goal.

Engage! A Guide to Involving Your Consumers in Their Health

You will need to get clearance from the individual first, but most will welcome the opportunity to be called out.

If you reward your consumers, take the opportunity to disseminate rewards that do not detract from your healthy living goals. Interestingly, many organizations are using "healthy lunches" as a reward. Move away from food as a reward (maybe a fruit gift basket is acceptable). You'll learn more about food, incentives, and rewards in separate chapters. For now, the message is simple: Take time to acknowledge successes, whether big or small.

By now you're probably thinking, "This is a lot of work!" You're right. Managing your health-care costs takes a great deal of effort on your part. But you don't have to undertake the process alone. You can ask for help from your broker, consultant, health plan representative, and any other business partners you engage in managing the health of your consumers. If these companies aren't providing you with the support you need, find someone who will.

With a reasonable investment of time, you'll be rewarded with better healthcare trends and happier consumers.

CHAPTER 3

Delivering the message
A year-long program to educate and engage consumers in their health

> *"An investment in knowledge pays the best interest."*
>
> – Benjamin Franklin

Education is not only the most critical component of engagement, but also a precursor to engagement. Without it, employees can neither begin to understand their responsibilities nor become an active participant in managing their healthcare. This chapter explores a variety of approaches and techniques that have proven effective at making employees more informed healthcare consumers.

Education versus communication versus engagement

The terms "education" and "communication" are often used interchangeably but they shouldn't be confused. Education implies that knowledge is being acquired while communication simply involves the dissemination of information (learning is optional). Furthermore, the fact that a consumer has learned something does not guarantee that he or she will take the

actions necessary to engage in the desired behavior. It's precisely this confusion that leads to a less-than-effective consumer engagement strategy. The implementation of a wellness program serves as an example of this.

The typical approach in a wellness program includes sending marketing collateral to consumers that describe the wonderful programs available. The brochure might even include what we (the employer, health plan, or provider) perceive to be the benefits of enrolling in a program. The "call to action" will be "sign up today!"

This is a mass-communication approach, in which the same generic message is used to reach all consumers. (And we wonder why this approach generates such low participation rates!) Mass communication doesn't guarantee the consumer has become educated, has engaged, or is ready to change his or her behavior.

It also does not guarantee that the consumer will even read the material. In all fairness to marketers, it's very difficult to engage people and get them excited. Relying on traditional marketing techniques is not going to create a culture of health. You will need to try some new techniques that may seem a bit unusual to catch the attention of your consumers. If you're considering hiring an external party (or even relying on an internal marketing or communications team), verify their understanding of the differences among education, engagement, and marketing and have them demonstrate how they plan to address all three areas for you.

It's also important to note that education doesn't happen only through reading the company benefits newsletter. Education happens during a workout at the on-site fitness center, in the break room, over lunch, in work-based chat rooms, and while talking across the desk with another employee. In other words, education can take place at any time. This is not to suggest that all written communications be tossed aside. These materials serve a purpose, which is to supplement the consumer's learning or serve as a reference.

Educate and communicate on a year-round basis

Education doesn't begin and end with open enrollment. A year-round strategy is vital to ensure that employees learn continuously. Let's walk through a typical plan year and review the various techniques used to educate consumers.

Prior to open enrollment

Education should begin prior to open enrollment and, depending on the ideas you plan to introduce, the process should begin as early as six months in advance. The discussion of numbers as mentioned in Chapter 2 is a good place to start. This context setting helps individuals become familiar with the healthcare-cost dilemma. If you've been sharing this information with your consumers on a regular basis, now is the time to summarize the prior plan year. Let individuals know what they've done to help mitigate the cost trend this year and where you continue to experience challenges.

From here, begin educating individuals on the plan options available to them during open enrollment. This initial discussion should be at a high level.

For example, focus on the rationale behind the introduction of a consumer driven plan, the elimination of a rich PPO plan, or a new requirement such as completion of a health risk appraisal as a condition for coverage. Setting the stage early on allows consumers to absorb information in small increments and increase their knowledge gradually. Lay the foundation now and build on it over time.

 Engage! A Guide to Involving Your Consumers in Their Health

Create an effective open enrollment campaign

Communication helps set the expectation for the open-enrollment process. Tradition involves mailing an open-enrollment kit to the home, which includes a cover letter from the CEO and a number to call for assistance. Many companies end the communication and engagement around open enrollment at this point. From their viewpoint, individuals know what to do. They read the information, check the premium contributions, determine whether point-of-service cost share has increased, and make a decision. This process is fine for those that believe this 15-minute assessment of coverage creates engagement. Believe me, it doesn't.

Under the scenario noted above, at least two-thirds of plan participants (and probably many more) will stay where they are. Some will not make a change because the cost share has not increased enough to warrant movement, and many others won't even take the time to look at the other options.

Make open enrollment a big deal

Open enrollment should be viewed as a major event for your organization and should focus on interaction among employees, the organization's leaders, and the human resources team. Benefits enrollment should be viewed and valued as an opportunity for engagement. It's a

time where individuals are focused on a single event, enrolling in their health benefits. During open enrollment, the dialogue will focus on the consumer's immediate needs: understanding options, evaluating cost and coverage, and choosing a plan. To maximize the value of the open-enrollment period, position this event as a launch pad to begin the dialogue that will continue for the remainder of the plan year.

Get the message right and be consistent

An effective communications and education strategy includes getting the message right. Too often, organizations rely on health plans or their brokers to set the tone for the open enrollment message. While these offers of assistance are appreciated, the message or theme for open enrollment must be established and communicated by the employer.

Delegating your message is akin to providing your plan administrator with a blank check. Owning the message does not prohibit you from having your broker, consultant, or health plan develop the communication and education materials or conduct open-enrollment meetings. It does mean that you will review and approve this information to ensure it is consistent with your message.

Great care should be taken to ensure that every aspect of the enrollment—from the benefits program name to the labels attached to the benefit plans and the decision support tools—all reflect the nature of the program. For example, the health insurance industry has adopted the term called high-deductible health plan (HDHP) simply because it is in the IRS regulations. Why would a consumer want to give any consideration to a plan that touts its key feature as a high deductible? Most consumers won't readily give up a $200 PPO deductible to take on a much higher cost share. This is why we as employers and health plans must do a better job of conveying the message we want these plans to send. One bank labeled its high-deductible plan as its "low-premium" plan and increased enrollment significantly over the prior year. In general, the plan labels do not provide any insight into what is different or distinguishing about the benefits. How is an employee to decipher the difference between PPO plan #1 and #2? Whether you are fully insured or self-funded, you can call the plans whatever you want. It may mean you have some extra work in creating the benefit plan materials, but if it results in a better consumer understanding of the healthcare options, it will be well worth the time and effort.

Naming the employee benefits program to reflect the organization's values serves as further reinforcement for employees. Dell's "Well at Dell" program sends a clear message to employees that health and wellness is an important company initiative. Create a name that incorporates your organization's values and you will further your mission to build and integrate a culture of health within your company.

Not the time for philosophy lessons

Once you move into the open-enrollment period, set expectations for consumers as to what the program will cover. If open enrollment is in process, it is not a good time to review the numbers and the drivers behind rising healthcare costs. Why? Because you've given your employees a limited time to make a decision, and they want details on plan design and cost share, period. Discussions on cost drivers or your philosophy around health benefits should occur in the months prior to open enrollment. This is why we recommend allowing up to six months in advance to begin the conversation with consumers around a health engagement strategy.

Make open enrollment a mandatory event
In addition to being a big event, open enrollment should be a mandatory event. One of the most important choices a consumer makes is the annual health plan election, yet most individuals spend very little time making this

©2007 HCPro, Inc.   Engage! A Guide to Involving Your Consumers in Their Health decision. Enrolling in a health plan is about as appealing to most consumers as completing their taxes. Despite the consumer's aversion to open enrollment, consumers should reexamine their choices and make a benefits election each year, including opting out of coverage. This approach, referred to as "positive enrollment," ensures that employees have their heads in the game. Positive enrollment helps combat the inertia that sets in when individuals are permitted to default to the same plan they had in the prior year. When an individual defaults to the same plan year after year, he or she loses the opportunity to reevaluate his or her healthcare needs on a regular basis.

If you have not previously required positive enrollment, start slowly by letting your employees know that failure to make an election will result in default to a specific plan design (which may not be the plan design they had the prior year). You may start with a middle-of-the-road plan the first year and then move to a high-deductible plan in subsequent years. Knowing they will not automatically get the prior year's plan will encourage individuals to participate in the process. Eventually, you can determine whether you want to be more aggressive and default the individual to no coverage if he or she fails to make an election. In the early years of implementation, always follow up with individuals that have not made an election to make them aware of the consequences of their actions.

Typically, it will be hard to get employees that are waiving other coverage to participate in the process at all. So don't expect that 100% of your employees will be actively involved.

Getting the coverage right

Thoroughly reviewing health plan options every year is important to ensure that each individual chooses the right amount of coverage. The employee may be required to choose among an HMO, PPO, or even a consumer-driven health plan. Considerations include the amount of the individual's premium contribution, deductibles, copays, and other cost share. With such heavy focus on the 47 million uninsured individuals in the United States, it's hard to believe that many consumers may be over-insured.

However, this is, in fact, the case with some individuals, and they may be leaving money on the table. For example, employees with working spouses who cover all family members under both plans may find that the additional premiums and the coordination of benefits provisions don't provide additional value relative to the cost. On the flip side, if the coverage between the two plans creates a feeling of 100% coverage, it may result in consumers unnecessarily using services. Some health plans recently experienced this phenomenon with high-deductible plans where coverage kicked in at 100% after the deductible was met. To maintain a balance between premium and point-of-service cost share, and encourage appropriate utilization, many agree that consumers should always be required to self-fund a portion of their healthcare.

Consumer healthcare needs may change from year to year. An individual who has used few services may be planning a major operation in the upcoming year and may want to buy a richer plan to lower overall out-of-pocket expenses or contribute additional funds to his or her health savings account to help cover the deductible.

Use tools to drive education

Open enrollment should focus on the choices consumers must make for their health benefits. Provide enough details so they can make informed decisions around premiums, plan cost share, and tax-advantaged accounts. To fully understand their total out-of-pocket costs, many individuals need help doing the math. Provide them with calculators and financial modeling tools that estimate their healthcare use for the upcoming year and the anticipated cost based on the plan design under consideration. These tools are often available free of charge through the health plan, third-party administrator, or your broker. Independent firms are also available to provide these services directly to employers.

Create examples of savings an individual can expect when contributing to a tax-advantaged account such as a flexible spending account or a health savings account. As your math teacher used to tell you in high school, show the work. These examples should be in the form of step-by-step calculations showing what the employee contributes annually and per pay period, as well as the tax savings. The idea of tax savings is too intangible for many individuals because they don't feel the benefit directly in their paychecks. Therefore, include comparisons to demonstrate the money left on the table after tax dollars are used. Doing the math for consumers makes it easier for them to understand what can be a complicated concept. Communications materials should allocate sufficient space to push the use of these tools because they lead to consumer education and engagement.

Engage! A Guide to Involving Your Consumers in Their Health

The human touch

In this world of electronic correspondence, many assume that these forms of communication are effective as the only means of communicating with and educating consumers. As discussed below, digital forms of communications can be used, but don't make the mistake of thinking they can replace human assistance. Until your employees are fully educated, you should retain a high level of human interaction during the open enrollment process, particularly if you are making a significant change in your health benefits offering. Benefits fairs and on-site meetings are effective means of educating individuals. Remember to invite spouses, who often manage the healthcare needs of the entire family. Telephonic support with extended hours is also critical to ensure employees can make contact after work when they are in the privacy of their own home. If the final days of open enrollment span a weekend, consider making your call center available for a limited time on Saturday.

Offer a peer-to-peer approach

Limited benefits staff and multiple locations make it difficult to provide the level of face-to-face interaction that we may prefer. When presented with these challenges, consider using a peer-to-peer approach as a supplement. This method involves training employees who are not part of human resources on your philosophy concerning the benefits offerings as well as plan details. Equipped with the education provided by the human resources staff, these individuals serve as ambassadors and advisors during the open enrollment period, offering additional, hands-on assistance to employees in need. These ambassadors are also available to new hires that lack the substantial support that is offered during the open enrollment process. A peer-to-peer approach allows consumers to have a conversation with someone who talks

with and relates to them on terms the average consumer can understand.

Hire an outside firm to provide specific expertise

Offering a high-deductible plan with a health savings account? Consider hiring external experts to advise employees as to whether to choose this plan and how to determine the amount they will contribute to their health savings accounts. One company that comes to the aid of consumers struggling to understand whether to choose a consumer-driven health plan option is MyFinancialAdvice, a financial planning advisory firm based in Boulder, CO. MyFinancialAdvice has developed a network of independent certified financial advisors that provide advice to consumers who are considering a consumer driven health plan option, such as a high-deductible health plan with a health savings account. For large companies, the financial advisors are trained on the company's benefits, including any contributions the organization has committed to make to the account. Employees can chat with the advisor online or over the phone. Companies like MyFinancialAdvice help ease the transition into and increase enrollment in consumer plans because consumers get the added touch of having a conversation about their benefits options with an experienced advisor.

Harness the power of technology

Take advantage of technology to reach a broad base of employees. Use Webcasts and the office intranet to reach remotely located employees. These techniques are inexpensive, but allow employees to feel connected to what's happening at the home office. For those individuals who miss a Webcast, make a copy available for replay during the open-enrollment period. Better yet, push these recorded sessions. Employees are more likely to listen to the information if it is sitting in their e-mail and they don't have to chase it down. If they can view or listen to the information at their convenience, they may be more likely to include their spouse or significant other in the process.

When deploying electronic communications, think about the technology your employees use.

If they don't have access to computers at work, allow them to sign up to receive information via their personal e-mail address at home. Don't assume that those who do not have access to or use a computer at work don't have access at home. Many individuals have and use computers at home (especially those with school-age children). To cover all bases, however, place kiosks throughout your locations for easy access to information. Touch-pad kiosks may be more effective than traditional computers for a population that isn't computer savvy. Since these devices are appearing at grocery stores and in airports, it is likely that your employees already have some familiarity with them.

If a large portion of individuals use hand-held devices, ensure that the educational tools and communications can be readily viewed from these devices. Cell phones still appear to be underutilized as a means to reach out to employees, especially for employers with a highly mobile population. Text messages can remind employees to get preventive care services, enroll in a health plan, or use a lower-cost drug.

These services are virtually untapped, but have the power to revolutionize the way we engage individuals in their health. As we will discuss in a subsequent chapter, cell phones may be an effective way to reach and engage younger consumers.

'Don't overload me'

While it may be hard to imagine, you can over communicate to your consumers. When this happens, they begin to tune out and stop responding to the communications. Create a year-round communications calendar that begins well before the open-enrollment period and continues through the remainder of the plan year. Creating this calendar ensures that communications are timed appropriately and spread out to prevent overload. The calendar should include all communications touch points, such as on-site meetings. Also, include communications that other areas of your organization may want to send to employees throughout the year. For example, you may have a series of wellness reminders scheduled for periodic release or an upcoming product launch. While you can't foresee all communications needs for the organization for the next 12 months, careful planning can help you minimize the amount of communications your consumers receive.

Maximizing benefits after open enrollment

As we stated before, education doesn't end at open enrollment. The education process must continue year-round to ensure individuals are constantly learning and growing into savvy healthcare consumers. Once the open enrollment process has ended and individuals have received their new health plan identification cards, focus on helping employees maximize the use of their health benefits throughout the year. Maximizing health benefits doesn't encourage inappropriate use of healthcare services; rather, it ensures that individuals who use services can maximize their coverage, especially in the case of limited benefits such as physical therapy services. Benefits maximization also helps individuals save money. In return, the employer will also save.

How do you then help your consumers maximize their benefits? Remind them to use network providers, seek care from their primary care physician at a lower cost, and create lists of minor and urgent care clinics that offer convenience and low cost. Include the telephone number for the nurse advice line on the identification card and in the member materials. Resurface the refrigerator magnets and the self-care handbooks. These tools serve as a means to reinforce self-help as an alternative to the emergency room for minor services. Tell consumers where they can find a free blood pressure machine so they can stretch their return visits to the provider if they self-report their findings on a regular basis. Attention healthcare providers: Think about putting a free blood pressure unit in the waiting room of your office and have it automatically download to your medical record. The consumer self-serves and gives you the opportunity to monitor his or her health without squeezing in another patient.

Hospital costs usually constitute a major portion of your healthcare expenditures. Consumers should be concerned with and diligent in choosing a hospital when contemplating an elective procedure. While the traditional doctor referral is still the most relied upon means for selecting the hospital, new tools are available to give individuals independent third party information on the hospital's performance. Quality and cost comparison tools provide information on costs for services ranging from a routine office visit to a hospital stay. Other indicators, such as the volume of procedures and morbidity and mortality rates, are available for hospital-based services. These indicators provide consumers with objective, industry-standard measures on which to evaluate local hospitals. Most tools also incorporate subjective criteria, such as proximity to the patient's home, to ensure that the evaluation goes beyond cost. While still not widely used, these tools are becoming more prevalent, particularly as plan designs eliminate copays and subject these services to deductibles and coinsurance. Ask your broker or plan administrator to hold a "lunch and learn" session to

educate employees on the availability of these tools.

Ongoing education on the use of lower-cost medications is critical to ensure that you catch individuals in the early stages of treatment. Check with your plan administrator to see how they reach out to consumers for appropriate medication use as well as ensuring compliance with medication plans. Have discussions around pill splitting, and make simple online tools available for employees and their dependents to locate lower-cost drug alternatives.

Putting it into practice

When we think about helping a consumer maximize his or her health benefits, we would typically look to the employer, broker, or the health plan. However, one healthcare provider that has been helping consumers maximize their benefits turned the tables and used the same philosophy with its own employees. As a provider of healthcare services, the employees at Discover Vision Centers in Kansas City, KS, are in a unique situation. These employees help consumers understand their vision benefits on a daily basis. CEO Jim Denning used these interactions to help his employees understand the trade-offs in their own health benefits. "Because we are in the healthcare business, our

 Engage! A Guide to Involving Your Consumers in Their Health

employees understand how insurance works. They see firsthand that patient expectations are higher when the insurer or employer is footing the bill. When the patient is paying a large portion or the full cost of the service, he or she is more willing to engage in a dialogue and explore lower-cost treatment alternatives that will have the same impact as a more expensive treatment," he said. Denning has seen the discussion around cost shift over the years. "The topic of cost used to be taboo, but now these discussions are on the table. Employees understand they have a deductible or a copay and will share in all or a part of the cost of the service. I don't know whether it's good or it's bad, but the cost discussion is happening."

Helping consumers maximize their benefits helps educate and engage them in their health and can lead to savings for consumers, employers, and providers alike. The examples provided just begin to touch the tip of the iceberg. Review your benefit plan and your consumers' healthcare needs and develop a plan to help them get the most from their health benefits.

The following is a summary of the communication, education, and engagement tips outlined in this chapter:

1. Don't rely on traditional mass-communication techniques to create consumer engagement or learning.

Think outside the box and come up with creative ways to communicate, educate, and engage.

2. Education occurs when consumers interact and learn from each other. Reading the benefits newsletter does not result in education.

3. Education is a year-round process and should begin as far as six months in advance of the new plan year.

4. Own your messaging and integrate it throughout all aspects of the open enrollment.

5. Make open enrollment a big deal and require a positive open enrollment.

6. Position the open enrollment period as a launch pad for year-round employee engagement.

7. Push the use of tools, e.g. calculators, as a means to educate and engage consumers.

8. Use digital technologies as another way to reach and engage consumers.

9. But don't lose the human touch. Ensure that employees can turn to a knowledgeable individual for assistance when needed.

10. Help consumers maximize their benefits by providing cost-saving tips, access to tools, and information.

11. Be careful not to overload consumers with too much information. Create a calendar of messages for the plan year.

Refer to Figure A.3, Figure A.4, Figure A.5, and Figure A.6 in the Appendix for additional materials related to this chapter.

Getting to know you

Simple techniques for gathering data and creating customized communications

> *"The best vision is insight."*
>
> – Malcolm Forbes

Society is overloaded with messages and information. Today's consumer skims through endless e-mails, sorting out the spam from the "must read." Junk mail is tossed in the circular file without a second thought. Technology allows consumers to bypass television commercials and view shows and movies at their leisure. Consumers have created a communications barrier that allows them to filter what they read, see, and hear. They're in control, and they decide which communications will make it over the wall.

Communications from employers or health plans won't be treated any differently. Therefore, we must find approaches that will capture and hold the consumer's attention. In this chapter, we'll explore several concepts that will help us more effectively target and engage consumers.

Tailor messaging to similar individuals

Targeted messaging refers to providing information that is relevant to a group of individuals with similar characteristics. Groups can be based on specific characteristics, such as diabetes, gender, or plan design. They can also be based on product features, such as contributions to a health savings account. Creating these groups or segments benefits the communications strategy in several ways.

Filtering out those consumers to whom the message is not relevant saves money and resources. And it might save your relationship with the consumers. Consumers are annoyed by communications that are not relevant and may question your organization's capabilities if they become inundated with information that is of no use to them. Good segmentation allows the message to be refined and therefore more meaningful to the recipient. When the consumer believes the message to be relevant, he or she will take the time to read it. Ideally, an employee who is currently enrolled in a traditional PPO plan should receive different communication materials than what is delivered to those who have already migrated to a consumer-driven health plan. The messaging to an individual who has previously enrolled in and completed a wellness program would differ from a message provided to individuals who have never enrolled in a wellness program, or who have enrolled in a program but did not complete it. Targeting helps eliminate the excess information and helps to establish a trusting relationship between you and your consumer.

Gather the data

Many organizations are not aware that they already have the data and, in many cases, the systems needed to create targeted messaging. The type of data needed to target your consumers can be very simple and may include gender, age, plan type the individual has chosen, work location, or home address. Generating a simple query into your systems can allow you to use more than one data attribute to create a customized e-mail or mailing list. For example, if mobile mammography will be available in a

certain location, you will want to notify all females age 40 and older who live or work near the service site. If you are unsure whether you can get to the information, check out your payroll or human resources system to determine which capabilities exist. Most off-the-shelf database packages contain a feature that allows you to generate these reports quickly and efficiently. If your system does not contain a reporting feature, refer to your information technology staff. They may be able to assist you in extrapolating the data into a simple Excel spreadsheet, which you can manipulate to produce electronic mailing lists or paper labels. The following are some examples of effective targeted messaging.

Health spending accounts – Target employees who have not contributed to a flexible spending or health savings account. Your company maintains a record of who is participating and who is not, as well as the amount elected. During the open enrollment period, send employees who are not making contributions a message that helps them understand the benefits of the account. In the message, include the math to illustrate the tax savings. Those employees who are already contributing to one of these accounts may only need a gentle reminder to continue contributing and revisit the amount of their contribution to maximize their tax savings. As you approach the end of your plan year, you (or your plan administrator) might send a notice to employees that have a balance remaining and explain which services can be paid for with funds from the account.

Preventive services – Often, an organization will rely on an annual calendar to educate individuals on the need for preventive services. While these are helpful reminders, individuals get these services at different times throughout the year. If a consumer receives a message to get a mammogram one month after she has received the service, it is of little benefit (and great annoyance) to her. Instead, send reminder notices of the preventive services an individual should be receiving 30–60 days after the service was due but not received. This time frame ensures ample time for a claim to be submitted and processed by the health plan to ensure you are not reminding someone who has already received the services.

Program participation – Targeted messaging is an effective way of getting your consumers to take notice of the programs and services you offer. Examples where targeted messaging may be effective include:

+ Driving smokers into smoking cessation programs

+ Reminding frequent emergency room users about the nurse call line service or providing information on the location of convenient care clinics

+ Increasing usage of your fitness center for those whose visits have fallen off

Also, your care management vendors should be using targeted messaging for their disease management programs. Alert an individual who has completed one wellness program that another program that might be of interest.

Prescriptions – Send messages to individuals who use brand-name drugs to encourage lower-cost alternatives. Contact individuals who take maintenance medications to encourage use of mail-order services.

Administrative functions – When an employee's dependent reaches the age where he or she may no longer be covered, send a notice to ask the employee to remove the child from coverage. Sending this reminder will let employees know you are tracking this information; knowing this, they are more likely to be honest. Use targeted messaging to remind those that have not enrolled that the deadline is approaching.

These examples sound simple, and many of us assume these are more prevalent than they actually are. Check with your plan administrator and verify that these methods are being used, and with regular frequency. In addition, work with your health plan to lay out a plan for targeted messaging as part of your overall communications plan. Targeted messaging can be in the form of phone calls (using voice-activated technology), e-mails, notes on paychecks, or traditional mail. Tailor the message to these groups to further ensure that the consumer receives relevant, meaningful information. Targeted messaging not only provides your consumers with a valuable service, it can also create a "teachable moment," a point of contact that has the potential to increase their healthcare education.

Customizing communications

Most organizations can't fathom creating separate communications for their consumers. The coordination could prove to be complicated and even costly. However, there is good news! In some situations, targeted messaging can be embedded within broader-based communications. For example, all employees may receive the same open enrollment kit explaining the company's three health benefits options: two traditional PPOs and a consumer driven health plan (CDHP). However, within the enrollment kits are scenarios consumers can read. Ideally

the consumer will identify and use the scenario with which they most closely relate as a starting point to move forward and make their decision. Scenarios can be based on the consumer's current plan design, coverage status (single, married, family), income, or health needs.

Using the aforementioned plan design as a basis, let's review an example. Envision two columns, one that states "If you are currently enrolled in PPO 500 or PPO 750…" and the other that states "If you are enrolled in HSA 1500…" The discussion in the PPO column will focus on looking at the total cost of care, including the employee's paycheck contributions. It may also include a comparison to the HSA-based plan to increase familiarity with it. The employee who has already made the switch to the HSA plan will typically not need a primer on how it works, nor will he or she need a comparison to the PPO.

However, employees with an HSA-based plan may need additional education on contributions and tax implications, as well as cost-saving tips. Starting the dialogue in this way will help them move along the continuum toward the desired plan and health choices.

     Engage! A Guide to Involving Your Consumers in Their Health

Personalized statements

Many large health insurers are now deploying a targeted messaging approach through personalized health statements. Similar to a banking or credit card statement, these summaries include the use of health services, suggest cost-saving tips, and include pertinent health information. Statements may be provided at a family or individual level and are provided periodically (typically monthly or quarterly). Messages are customized to the individual's specific health condition, increasing the likelihood that the individual will read the information. For example, coupons for a lower-cost over-the-counter allergy alternative may be included in the statement for an individual using a prescription antihistamine, while an individual taking a brand-name drug will receive information on the quality and cost savings associated with a generic medication. Customized messages can be generated to individuals who may be eligible for flu shots with a list of the locations where the individual can obtain the shot.

Due to the highly personalized nature of these statements, this form of communication is likely to replace the traditional, broad-based newsletters that cover many issues that may or may not be of use to the consumer. For example, a young mother does not want to filter through pages of classes for seniors rather, she wants to review information that is applicable to her lifestyle. Ask your health plan if a personalized statement is available for your consumers and whether messages can be customized based on the specific health needs of your population.

Healthcare providers might consider how they can take advantage of this concept as well. Instead of sending a broad-based newsletter to all consumers residing in your service area, consider purchasing household data and creating customized newsletters based on age, income, and gender. By tailoring this information, consumers will not only pay attention, your organization will come to their mind the next time they need services.

The generation gap

Understanding the mindsets of different generations is important in comprehending how individuals view their health. Knowing how members of different generations relate to and use the healthcare system or how they adopt technology can help determine the best strategy and approach to take in educating and engaging consumers. "Our grandparents' generation paid for their own healthcare. There were no expectations that someone else would pay for their care. They used the healthcare system wisely and in many cases they were healthier than we are," states Barb Thode of Orion Corporation.

Workforces are diverse in ethnic and racial background, income, and educational level. However, an equally strong influence on healthcare use will be the generational mix of your consumers. "Today's senior population view physicians and other healthcare professionals with reverence," comments Dianne Kiehl with BHCG, the Business Health Care Group of Southeast Wisconsin. "This view causes them to accept what they're told and not to question the information provided." When the patient views the healthcare professional as all-knowing, he loses his ability to be as active as he needs to be in managing his own healthcare needs. He may not ask for treatment alternatives or lower-cost prescriptions to save on out-of-pocket expense. This lack of understanding is correlated with compliance. It's difficult for the consumer to comply without understanding the reason behind the treatment. With over 35 million individuals age 65 or over in the United States, the hesitance to have a dialogue with a physician can have a tremendous impact on healthcare costs.

The boomers' view

The baby boomer generation, which includes individuals born between 1946 and 1964, have made an impact in many areas over the years and health is no different. Boomers are more likely to take control of and be engaged in their health than their parents. Boomers still view physicians with respect, but they are more inclined to engage in a dialogue with the physician; question recommendations; and seek additional information, including second opinions. Boomers view themselves as being in charge of their health. This attitude drives a high level of engagement which, in turn, leads to more informed healthcare decisions. An organization with a high number of boomers should be prepared to provide these individuals with access to information on costs, provider credentials, and treatment alternatives. Boomers will want to look at the total picture before making a decision. In addition, boomers, unlike seniors, are looking outside the local area for healthcare. These individuals are likely to be willing to travel to have services provided at the best facility or by the best provider. The belief that healthcare is local is slowly eroding. Healthcare providers are now competing with providers in other states and other countries. Read more about the concept of "medical tourism" in Chapter 5.

Gen X and Gen Y

Members of generation X (gen Xers) and generation Y (the millennial generation or "millennials") are a whole new ballgame. Gen Xers were born after the boomers between

1965 and 1976. In an article from the November 2005 issue of *Law Practice Today*, the authors Diane Thielfoldt and Devon Scheef share that GenXers "are practical and self-reliant . . . They reject rules and have a basic mistrust of institutions" (which includes employers, healthcare providers, and health plans). The millennial generation moves to the next level. According to Thielfoldt and Scheef, "They don't simply reject the rules, they rewrite them. They move beyond institutional mistrust to the realm of irrelevance. They even leap over their predecessors and assume technology as a key part of most any activity."

When interacting with the healthcare system, these individuals will ask questions, seek alternatives, and come to their own conclusions. They'll use healthcare professionals as advisors rather than the final authority, and technology will be a factor in decision-making. Communicating with and educating these individuals may require a shift from one of content provider to that of facilitator. Gen Xers and millennials want to review all the information and all the evidence on a particular service or treatment prior to making a decision. In addition, they will incorporate a cocreation model where other consumers pass on their knowledge and recount their experiences. All these elements will factor into the decision-making process. The employer, provider, and health plan will simply be one source of input

and not a source for definitive information. Use of the latest technology will be a requirement for these generations. These consumers will want information on demand. Today, many health activists provide content to consumers via employer intranets and provider and health plan Web sites. This content is typically provided by a single, independent third-party resource such as WebMD. The content is static, and the consumer is a passive participant in this process. Health plan and medical content Web sites as they exist today will change. The consumers will determine which portion of a Web site they value and then pull relevant health information into their self-constructed home page.

Why is it important to understand these generational differences? According to Dianne Kiehl, "Gen Xers and the millennials think differently, and as they begin to take care of their aging parents, their communication and learning styles will have a rapid and meaningful impact on the healthcare system." Without this knowledge, education and communications campaigns will fail. Communications must be able to reach and engage consumers that fall into each of these segments. Telling an aging senior to surf the Internet and use the information to enter into a discussion with his or her physician will likely be met with disbelief and perhaps even indignation. Conversely, providing paper communications only to employees in their twenties or asking them to come to your Web site as a single source of authority will result in a rebuff. Without understanding the generational influences of consumers, your education and engagement strategy may miss the mark.

A new approach

As adults, we know we should change some of our health behaviors. The cigarette packaging tells us the ramifications of smoking and we know being overweight leads to a variety of chronic diseases and illnesses. We read, listen, and then move on, ignoring what we know to be true. Why, as educated adults, do we ignore the information and warning signs? We may ignore these signals because they are not in sync with our attitudes and beliefs toward health. Consumers engage in their health on their own terms. Communications must be customized and personalized in order to create engagement. Yet most communication strategies strive for the lowest common denominator and assume this approach will engage everyone at some level. The reality is that few consumers find the information relevant and even fewer are engaged.

The mass-communication approach must be replaced with a strategy that incorporates how individuals engage in their health, including how they interpret and process the information

we provide them. Why does this matter? Once we understand how people learn we can then talk with and treat them in a way they expect and welcome. In addition, the way an individual engages in his or her health can drive utilization.

 A small company known as the Path Institute has developed nine personas around how people engage in their health. "Each persona has characteristically different ways in dealing with and engaging with their health with well-documented impacts on disease prevalence and health costs," states Sandra Leal, a consultant with The Concours Group, who works with the Path Institute. "Using these personas, an employer can begin to identify and then address the health priorities behaviors and attitudes of its employees that are driving healthcare outcomes and engagement." The personas cover a broad spectrum and include, for example, "ready users," who frequently access the healthcare system; "traditionalists," who come with their own preconceived notion of healthcare; and "naturalists," who show some interest in alternative remedies.

By answering a series of questions, a consumer can be identified and classified into one of nine categories. This category can then be tagged to the consumer's file in the same way a date of birth or an address is linked. Imagine using this tag to create customized content to support an employee benefits or wellness program. The messaging sent to an individual who avoids the healthcare system at almost any cost would vary greatly from that sent to someone who is more traditional and likely to follow the doctor's instructions to a tee. The one-size-fits-all approach would be replaced with an education and communications plan that addressed the learning needs of employees based on their attitudes toward health.

With the assistance of The Concours Group, the Path Institute is testing the use of these personas in a large Midwest hospital system with the intent to create a different ambulatory consumer experience. Focused approaches such as these will help drive competitive differentiation and advantage for healthcare providers. As

employers and health plans grow increasingly sophisticated in determining provider network participation and corresponding payment rates, demonstrating the ability to help consumers create healthy lifestyles may result in higher payments or volume of patients.

Getting to know your consumers will help you focus your outreach and engagement strategies to gain the maximum benefit. Progress can be made with simple steps, such as using basic demographic information to create customized messages and campaigns. Consumers are more likely to read and respond to these strategies when the information provided is relevant to them. Gain an understanding of your consumers and use it to create an effective communications campaign.

Design details

Recommendations for designing a health plan that helps—not hinders—your engagement goals

> *"America's healthcare system is neither healthy, caring, nor a system."*
>
> – Walter Cronkite, legendary television journalist

Health insurance coverage began as a means to attract and retain employees. For most employers, offering health benefits is a requirement, a necessity to compete. When weighing competitive offers, the comprehensiveness of the health benefits is a major influencing factor for most consumers. Yet it is the health benefits, the very thing an organization must have, that puts significant strain on organizations. Many factors drive the increase in healthcare costs, including utilization of services, unit costs, new technology, and pharmaceuticals.

Over the years, many employers would say they have cut back on their health benefits. In reality more healthcare services are covered now than were covered five to 10 years ago. Consider some of the introductions of new medical services or procedures over the last several decades, including joint replacements, Viagra, laparoscopic procedures, CAT scans,

MRIs, Nexium, and more. Today, consumers learn about new products and services while they're still in development and eagerly anticipate their arrival.

If a U.S. government entity states that a service can be performed or distributed, consumers believe it should be covered under their health benefits. For the most part, employers and health plans are responding to these desires. The waiting period between when a new procedure or service is introduced to the mass market and the time it's deemed to be a covered benefit is growing increasingly shorter.

In addition, many lifestyle-related services are covered as part of the benefit plan. Even though deductibles and copays have risen over the years, the coverage of more services and increases in costs and utilization cause health cost to increase at double the rate of other indices.

The benefit plan design can be used to help control some of the drivers of health costs. The underlying plan design has been, and continues to be, a vehicle to direct individuals, when appropriate, to lower-cost or more efficient alternatives. Cost share differentials like deductibles, copays, and coinsurance guide individuals to the use of participating providers and to centers of excellence in the case of catastrophic events. These same cost features are used to encourage use of lower-cost medications, technologies, or places of service (e.g., outpatient versus inpatient). With the constant influx of new services into the health system, the employer has to be diligent in ensuring the plan design is keeping pace with the times.

Inertia is the enemy

Many employers have employed some of the features discussed above; however, after the change is made, the plan design remains static for a period of time thereafter with changes only to the premium contribution. When the status quo is maintained in the plan design, inertia sets in, and inertia is an employer's worst enemy. To combat inertia, the plan design must change each year. Changes, even the smallest ones, will cause consumers to reevaluate their benefits each year. When nothing changes, consumers tend remain in their current plan. In addition, when the plan designs don't change, the employee has no reason to think about how

he or she is using healthcare. Every plan, every year, needs to change. The following are some of the key plan-design features that can be used to change behavior that you can use to drive consumer decision-making.

Restructure office visit copays

If the plan design covers office visits for a copay, create a meaningful differential between primary care and specialist physician services. Eliminate single office visit copays for any physician type. Specialists typically drive proportionally more of the healthcare costs than do primary-care physicians and the consumer cost share should increase accordingly.

Encourage individuals to seek care from their primary care doctors first by applying a lower copay for these providers. The copay differential should be between $15 and $20, enough to cause the consumer to think twice, but not so much as to place undue burden on individuals that require specialist services.

Employees should be encouraged to select a primary-care physician at the time of enrollment, even when they are not joining an HMO. While this selection is optional, it reinforces the importance of establishing a relationship with a personal physician, which continues to be an essential component to helping manage healthcare costs.

Use copay differentials to direct urgent or convenient care

Most plan designs use copays for steerage of other provider services beyond physician office visits. Copay differentials can be highly effective in driving use of urgent care centers or convenient-care clinics in lieu of emergency rooms for nonemergency situations. Some hospitals use the urgent-care label, but bill at the same rate as the emergency room, which means your consumers will seek care at these facilities and assume they are following the rules. But the plan will not reflect any savings. If you include this feature in the plan design, provide your consumers with a list of clinics that fall into the urgent- or minor-care category, as well as those that do not.

Ensure efficient care with per-day copays

Copays-per-admission are a standard means of ensuring that outpatient treatment is reviewed as an alternative when appropriate. If an admission is warranted, once the copay is paid, the patient and his or her family no longer have a financial incentive to ensure that care is provided efficiently. Since many health plans no longer have on-site nurses, the patient may encounter delays in receiving necessary tests or services, such as therapy. Shifting to a copay-per-day system can provide the individual with an appropriate incentive to ensure he or she is getting the care he or she needs in a timely manner. Paying an extra $100 per day will help the consumer become his or her own advocate

will encourage discussion with the doctor around appropriate timing of discharge, as well as the use of home support services such as home health nursing. Cap the number of days the copay applies to in order to avoid creating a hardship for your employees and their family members.

Incorporate pharmacy cost sharing

Healthcare consumers often have an expectation that each visit to the doctor should include a prescription as the cure. They're surprised when they arrive at the pharmacy and discover the amount they're expected to pay.

Pharmacy management programs have included several techniques for getting individuals to switch to lower-cost medications, use mail-order services, or comply with the prescribed therapy. Design features include waiving or lowering copays and issuing coupons for over-the-counter alternatives.

Other approaches are more restrictive: mandating generics over brand medications and use of mail-order for chronic medications. Prescription drugs are usually placed into multiple tiers based on either brand-name versus preferred generic or cost. Creating a tiered plan design (three-tier minimum) based on cost allows more flexibility in ensuring that employees and dependents use lower-cost medications that are equally as effective as those with higher costs, whether brand or generic.

Introduce allowance-based plans

Several health plans have introduced allowance-based plans. The plans have limited success in the volume of sales; however, they appear to create real behavior changes. Allowance plans eliminate copays and establish a set amount for the entire class of drugs. The allowance amount typically varies by drug class. The allowance amount may be based on the median price in a certain drug class or may be calculated to ensure that the majority of drugs in the class are lower than, equal to, or only slightly above the allowance. The allowance setting ensures the consumer is provided with plenty of low-cost alternatives. Allowance plans make the true cost of the drug transparent to the individual and encourage shopping behaviors because, in many cases, the consumer has the option to get the medication for free or at a significantly lower cost by requesting either a lower-cost brand or a generic alternative.

Create a separate specialty pharmacy benefit

Specialty pharmacy is a high-growth area in terms of cost and volume. These medications are typically geared toward serious illnesses and are significantly more expensive than non-specialty pharmaceuticals. These medications may be in the injectable or oral form and should be reviewed and assessed annually as a distinct benefit within the plan design. Health plans work with a number of specialty pharmacy vendors to obtain these medications at a significantly reduced cost when compared to the price of the drug at a retail pharmacy or a physician's office, where large mark ups are the norm. The drugs can be delivered to the consumer's home or to the doctor's office.

Most plan designs today lump specialty pharmacy in with the traditional pharmacy, medical plans, or both. The consumer pays a copay at the pharmacy or to the physician when the medication is provided in the office. These small copays (relative to the cost of the drug) don't create an incentive to use lower-cost providers. Therefore, consider establishing a separate specialty pharmacy benefit design that steers the consumer (some plan designs mandate use of specialty providers) to these lower-cost sources, yet maintains the convenience to which the consumer is accustomed and does not interrupt the patient-physician relationship.

Integrate incentives and rewards

A trend is emerging that integrates incentives and rewards into benefit plan design. This approach typically comes in two forms. One is to allow entry into a plan with lower cost-share with the assumption that the individual will engage in the desired activities throughout the year. If the individual does not comply, he or she is moved to a plan with a higher cost-share, either at some point during the plan year or at the beginning of the next plan year.

A criticism of these plans is that the reward may not feel as tangible to the individual. For example, if the consumer can stay in the lower-cost plan for an entire year without engaging in the desired behaviors, he or she may not be as motivated to engage. On the other hand, if the individual is a high utilizer of services and is now in a lower-cost share plan, he or she may be very engaged from the beginning. The other plan design provides the employee with reward dollars, rebates in the form of deductible credits, or contributions to a health account based on completion of desired behaviors. Under these plan designs, the more a consumer performs activities, the more rewards or credits are earned. Some of these plan designs provide credits or rewards based on health outcomes. Refer to Chapter 7 for examples of plan design-based and other rewards programs.

Consider consumer-driven health plans

Consumer-driven health plans can be an effective means to engage employees, but like any of the other features mentioned in this chapter, they are not a solution in and of themselves. These plans are good at getting consumers to begin to understand the cost of care by eliminating copays and subjecting all nonpreventive services to a deductible. This plan design creates a true sense of transparency. The fact that the consumer has some financial cost share at stake motivates him or her to engage in a dialogue with his or her physicians and seek out lower-cost medications and treatments when appropriate.

Detractors of these plan designs fear that consumers will not get the care they need due to the financial impact. The majority of employers couple these plan designs with a funded health account that helps to offset the deductible and can be used for medications as well. It's important to provide consumers with tools to help them do the math so they can fairly evaluate the financial impact of a consumer-driven plan versus a traditional HMO or PPO plan. When all costs are considered, including employee premium contributions and copays (which typically do not apply to the out-of-pocket maximum), many consumers may find that these consumer plans may help them save over the plan year. However, consumers are used to cost share in smaller increments and may need some assistance in understanding how to budget for their healthcare expenses.

Establish embedded deductibles

When qualified high-deductible plans were first introduced, the family deductible was aggregated. This means the entire family deductible must be satisfied before any nonpreventive benefits are payable by the plan. These aggregate deductible plans do not provide protection in the event that a single individual within the family incurs significant costs. Offering an embedded deductible provides the consumer with additional peace of mind while adding minimal cost to the plan. This feature also allows consumers to make an apples-to-apples comparison with traditional PPO plans. Having an aggregate deductible in the consumer-driven plan and an embedded deductible in the traditional plan will hurt migration to the consumer plans.

Fund health savings account

Employers must seed the account if they are offering a health reimbursement arrangement, but are not obligated to do so with a health savings account. While funding the account has its pros and cons, seeding the account will generally help drive more consumers into the high-deductible plan. In addition, employees may be more likely to contribute their own funds to the account when the employer also contributes. Over the long term, the desire is to get the consumer to contribute to the account to fund short- and long-term healthcare expenses. If the employer continues to fund a flat amount into the account regardless of the consumer's participation, the consumer may become less engaged over the long term.

To combat this potential apathy, some employers are funding these accounts based on incentives and rewards. The employee or a dependent has to take an action such as completing a health risk appraisal or participating in a disease management program to earn the contribution (read more in Chapter 7). In another twist, Humana launched a matching contribution strategy for its employees based on salary level. Humana matched the individual's contribution, providing a higher match to some employees and no match to employees at the highest salary levels and included an overall single and family cap. "We felt this approach would really engage our employees and encourage them to contribute to their health savings accounts. We believe it is important for individuals to self-fund a portion of their routine healthcare expenses and this approach motivates them to do just that while ensuring that some employees have a greater opportunity to maximize Humana's company match," states Deborah Triplett, director of benefits and human resources policy for Humana.

Investigate value-based plan designs

Value-based plan designs are beginning to surface within the industry. These plan designs focus on removing financial barriers to care for specific diseases or conditions. Examples include Pitney Bowes' plan design to ensure access to diabetic drugs and supplies and the Ashville Project, designed to overcome financial barriers to medication compliance (it also includes a coaching component). Why are these programs important? Cost may be a deterrent to medication compliance. In addition, some conditions don't carry immediate symptoms that serve as a constant reminder to continue medication adherence. The lack of symptoms and financial barriers may result in individuals failing to follow their medication regimen. Value-based plan designs are structured to overcome these challenges and result in improved health outcomes. While value-based plan designs have been focused primarily on prescription services, these concepts can be transferred to other services, as well. When considering a value-based plan design, include a coaching component to generate sustainable behavior change.

Qualified high-deductible plans also permit preventive medications prior to the deductible. Look at the major conditions in your employee population and decide whether it makes sense to exempt certain medications prior to the deductible. You can choose to put cost share on these medications, such as a copay or coinsurance, but all consumer cost share must be applied to the out-of-pocket maximum.

Ensure preventive-care services remain covered

Recently, there has been some question as to whether high-deductible health plans cover preventive services. The vast majority of these plans, as well as traditional PPO and HMO plans, have covered, and will continue to cover, preventive services prior to the deductible at little to no cost share. A shift away from this

philosophy is not anticipated. Covering preventive care makes good business sense. Catching serious illnesses early, like cancer, not only saves the employer or health plan money, it saves lives, and plan designs should continue to encourage use of these services. Most plans cover routine exams, such as well-child visits, immunizations, and mammograms prior to the deductible; however, some still place an annual maximum payment on these services. While the majority of individuals will ensure their children get the needed preventive services, they may not be as vigilant in obtaining these services themselves when faced with high out-of-pocket expenses. Remove preventive care maximums from the plan design, as these maximums have little impact on plan costs in the short-term but can have significant impact on long-term costs. Consumers shouldn't be put in the position of having to trade off getting a mammogram or paying a utility bill.

Offer premium differentials

Premium differentials are used to steer consumers into the preferred plan as determined by the employer. Many consumer-driven plans may have the lowest price tag (or even be free) to the consumer to drive adoption. Salary differentials are a way of ensuring that lower-income individuals have access to affordable, comprehensive health coverage. This approach ensures that those that are more highly compensated subsidize the cost of care. Whatever approach you take, ensure there is a sufficient amount of premium differential to get consumers to stop and take a look at the preferred-plan design. When trying to create steerage, adjust the cost share on the nonpreferred plans in addition to the premium contribution to ensure your

employees get the message that there are other alternatives to consider. When the premium differential between the nonpreferred and preferred plans becomes so high that an individual would not benefit by taking the nonpreferred plan, it's time to eliminate the nonpreferred plan.

Emerging trend: "Medical tourism"

"Healthcare is local." This statement has been reiterated over and over by healthcare providers, consultants, employers, and health plans. Although those entities may not have changed their minds, some consumers have. The emergence of "medical tourism" is slowly beginning to alter the way we think about providing access to high-cost healthcare services.

The term "medical tourism" usually evokes the idea of undergoing cosmetic surgery and recovering in an exotic location with the ocean breeze and a drink with an umbrella on top. While this view has been correct in the past, the idea of medical tourism is changing.

Other countries have watched the United States, and in particular U.S. employers, struggle with the increasing costs of healthcare, and now they are offering—and aggressively promoting—solutions. Hospitals in Thailand, Singapore, and India, for example, are vying for U.S. citizens who are willing to travel to their countries to have heart bypass surgery, hip replacements, and other major procedures. These healthcare providers advertise state-of-the-art facilities and Western-trained physicians who will provide care of equal or higher quality than those in the States.

The cost of these international services may be half to one-third of the cost of the procedure in the United States—even when including round-trip airfare and lodging for the patient and a companion. Who might consider getting these types of services overseas? The uninsured, part-time workers with limited health benefits that only pay five to ten thousand a year for services and individuals in a high-deductible health plan. As family deductibles and out-of-pocket expenses approach $10,000, an individual may get ahead of the game by receiving care abroad. In addition, employers may consider offering medical tourism options to individuals covered under a traditional plan. Some health plans have stated they are covering these services at varying levels under their current benefit plans.

While the lower cost of care may seem attractive, it's important to note that some facilities may not be accredited and the patient may very well be on his or her own should complications arise once he or she has returned to the United States. Furthermore, while the facilities themselves may be state of the art, once outside the hospital, the patient and his or her companion may find themselves in underdeveloped, high-poverty areas, and they may be challenged with language barriers.

Many employers are not prepared to assist consumers who may be exploring these options. Employers must determine whether they want to offer assistance by financing the service or by merely providing information on the healthcare providers and organizations that are available to provide this care in other countries. Medical tourism is a trend to watch, however. If consumers are permitted to seek care anywhere in the U.S., why not expand that option to the anywhere in the world?

Typically, consumers believe that choices in plan designs consist of an HMO, PPO, and a consumer-driven plan. As employers make significant progress in migrating individuals into consumer-driven plans, and traditional plans are eliminated, employers fear that all other options for ongoing cost share will be eliminated. Organizations can continue to offer employees choices through deductible and funding options. In addition, the employer can review the plan's covered services or value-added options to create differentiation. Creating choices for consumers so they can choose the plan that best meets their financial and healthcare needs is another way to combat inertia.

CHAPTER 6

Redefining wellness
Using 'well'-designed programs to collect meaningful data and boost your enrollment numbers

> *"Healthy citizens are the greatest asset any country can have."*
>
> – Winston Churchill

The idea of consumer engagement is often associated with the implementation of a wellness program, but as we've seen, consumers can be engaged in many other ways, such as through education and plan design. However, wellness programs do play a significant role in consumer engagement since they are based on education and help drive healthy lifestyles. Wellness programs address common health issues, such as smoking cessation, stress management, and nutritional counseling, and these are topics that most consumers understand.

Standard components of wellness programs include health risk appraisals, smoking cessation, and weight management programs, to name a few. Biometric screenings along with health coaching have begun to emerge in recent years, as well. Increasingly, employers are adding features to their wellness programs that may be unique to their employee population.

This chapter will identify the core components of a wellness program along with some customized approaches created by employers, and it will explore how they engage consumers and improve their lifestyles.

Allen Johnson, chief administrative officer, Montgomery County Hospital District in Texas, acknowledges that wellness programs play an important role. "People want to be healthy, but many don't know how to get there, to get it all together. Wellness programs help individuals take the first step." Johnson knows what he's talking about. The wellness programs he has helped drive have created very positive results for his consumers. (We'll dig a little deeper into Johnson's programs later on in this chapter.)

Wellness programs aren't something new. In the past, most HMOs embraced these programs as a means to get members to change their lifestyles. Often referred to as "health education," these programs covered the aforementioned issues. The member may have been referred to the program by his or her primary-care physician or through self-referral. Early health education programs were held in classroom-like settings and met periodically. These early programs faced many challenges. They required face-to-face interaction with an instructor in a dedicated location. Using the traditional student/teacher approach, health education programs typically did not identify the consumer's readiness to change or differentiate learning styles among participants. In addition, the weekly meetings did not fit into many consumers' busy schedules, and the group approach didn't appeal to all. Wellness programs have come a long way since those early days with innovations designed to meet the consumers' needs, regardless of how varied those might be.

Begin with the health risk appraisal

The health risk appraisal serves as the foundation to a wellness program. This screening is typically completed by the individual online, via paper, or via an interactive voice response system. Health risk appraisals are designed to capture family history, lifestyle habits, and other information the health plan or plan administrator does not typically capture in

claims. Health plans may use the output from the appraisal to enhance their predictive modeling capabilities and drive referrals into their clinical programs. If you're using a stand-alone vendor for your health risk appraisal, ask if it can export the data to the health plan (and whether the health plan can accept it). If not, consider using the health plan's appraisal to gain the advantage of integration.

Consumers may view the health risk appraisal with some skepticism. They may worry that plan administrators will share their health information with their employers or use the results to raise premiums or possibly exclude them from coverage. The employer must reassure employees that the information is kept confidential and used appropriately. Participation in employer- and health plan-based health risk appraisals is increasing slightly, mostly through the use of incentives and rewards (see Chapter 7). Even with an incentive, employees may not understand the need to complete the appraisal. Lack of understanding may be driven by the confidentiality concerns or by the fact that the consumer simply doesn't see the value of completing the health risk appraisal. He or she has completed these assessments in the past and received standard content at the end telling him or her to lose weight, stop smoking, etc. Consumers don't view the health risk appraisal as educational (because they know what they should do) nor do they find it engaging. Consumers are right! Many health risk appraisals take 30 to 45 minutes to complete and are, quite frankly, boring.

Health risk appraisals have much opportunity for innovation, but there is one appraisal out there that does create a good level of consumer engagement. In fact, it's so engaging that over 17 million individuals have completed this assessment and millions sign up for its related newsletters and tips. The Web site is *www.realage.com*. Founded by consumer health champion Dr. Michael Roizen, the RealAge test is engaging and different from most health risk appraisals because it calculates your "Real Age" as you answer questions. Don't exercise or floss your teeth regularly? Smoke or drink too much? These bad habits can contribute to your "Real Age" being greater than your actual age. Ouch! Conversely, having healthy habits can actually make you younger than your real age. Great!

Health insurers that offer medical coverage directly to consumers have essentially required a health risk appraisal on every individual applying for coverage as part of the underwriting process. Completion of a health questionnaire helps the health insurer determine the rate the consumer will be charged for health insurance. While this practice is commonplace in the individual market, it's not the norm in the group market. Because the group's health experience is reviewed collectively to determine the health insurance premium, with the exception of small employers, health insurers do not require completion of a health questionnaire by each employee. However, some employers have taken the approach that a health risk appraisal must be completed as an eligibility requirement to gain access to the employer's health coverage. Employers believe that completion of a health risk appraisal (typically only for the employee, but some also require the spouse to complete one) is a fair exchange for receiving an annual health benefit that costs thousands of dollars. Employees may see this requirement as a big-brother approach; however, most will comply, as they value their health benefits offering.

Offer core wellness classes

Lifestyle or behavior modification programs, such as nutrition or weight management, smoking cessation, back care, or stress management, are typically core pieces of a wellness program. Typically administered in the form of Internet-based self-service, consumers have access to content that describes the issue and presents a variety of approaches and programs, sometimes tailored to the consumer's needs. Online programs allow the individual to move at his or her own pace in an anonymous and convenient manner. While the newer versions of these programs do not require face-to-face classroom time, most programs do offer telephonic coaching services (usually at an additional fee to the employer or the consumer). The coach provides additional support and motivation to the individual to help ensure he or she will stay on track with his or her personalized improvement plan. These core programs are essential to a well-rounded program because they address the needs of a very large part of your consumer population. Changing your consumer behaviors based on core offerings could make a significant impact to the bottom line over time.

Provide support for chronic conditions

Disease management programs are also included in the wellness realm. These programs target individuals with chronic conditions, such as diabetes, asthma, and coronary artery disease. Often, they partner consumers with a nurse and other healthcare professionals to help them learn how to manage their health. Some benefit-plan designs are structured to require participation in disease management or coaching programs as a trade-off for maintaining lower deductibles and copays. The companies that administer these programs can typically demonstrate a reasonable return on investment, although the time periods may vary.

Disease management programs usually address illnesses that have the potential to be high-cost. Therefore, offering these programs is essential to a strong wellness program. Review your claims data to determine which of these programs you should be offering to your consumer population. Disease management programs may also be lumped into the category of care management programs. While a portion of these programs is designed to ensure that care is delivered efficiently, these programs should also have a strong focus on helping the individual adopt and maintain healthy behaviors. When assessing potential partners for these programs, understand whether their philosophy is strictly about managing costs or whether it also involves healthy behaviors.

Helping expectant moms

Pregnancy programs may be incorporated under the umbrella of disease management programs, but these initiatives deserve a special look. For organizations with young populations, the chances of high-risk pregnancies and premature births increase. When pregnant employees or dependents have access to a pregnancy program, it can make a real difference in increasing the likelihood of a healthy pregnancy and birth, which translates to tremendous savings for the employer and high satisfaction for the new mom. In particular, enrolling teenage moms into these programs can help these young adults learn how to take care of themselves and avert or minimize a premature birth.

For most individuals, having a baby is an exciting time, and pregnancy programs seize that opportunity to engage the moms-to-be. At Dell, participants in the pregnancy program receive a gift basket full of goodies for the baby (including merchandise with the Dell logo) and those in need have a coach to support and guide them through the pregnancy. Unless your consumer population skews well beyond the pregnancy years, ensure that your consumers have access to a pregnancy program.

Get your executives healthy

Executive health programs are typically offered to the senior management team and may involve a comprehensive physical and plan of action for improving the individual's health. Take a minute and visualize your senior management team. Are they the picture of health? Do their personal habits reflect a culture of wellness and are they a role model for your consumers to follow? There are probably a number of heads shaking "no."

The executive health program is important because it provides a means of engaging your leaders in wellness. Once they know their own numbers, they're more likely to embrace the concept of wellness and share their enthusiasm with employees.

Some organizations are offering a full executive health program. The program provides each executive with a complete annual physical exam and a personalized health program. While these programs may appear to come with a heavy price tag, consider the option of losing critical employee knowledge and productivity as a result of a serious illness that, if caught early, may have been controlled.

Have fun with health

Health fairs have been a staple in wellness programs for quite a while, but are evolving with the times. These fairs provide everything from blood pressure and cholesterol screenings to nutritional consults and healthy cooking demonstrations. Many vendors are available to choose from, but if you're on a budget, look no further than your own backyard. Many local healthcare providers, such as hospitals, pharmacies, and therapists, may be willing to provide services at the health fair either free of charge or for a nominal fee. These providers view the health fair as an opportunity to advertise their services. Discuss the terms of the health fair with the providers to ensure they won't be pushing their services on your consumers and generating unnecessary or inappropriate utilization. Don't forget to invite your consumers' spouses to the fair and use small prizes as enticements to get people to attend. For example, give out passports that consumers have stamped when they visit a health station. Those who fill the passport completely are eligible for a larger prize. Remember to conduct the health fair in a location that is easily accessible, e.g., near the cafeteria or in the auditorium.

Executive health programs can help protect an organization from this knowledge loss by ensuring its top management are either in good health or getting the assistance and care they need to manage a condition.

Help consumers learn their numbers

Biometric screenings are increasingly more prevalent in wellness programs today than they were five years ago. Biometric screenings are used to educate consumers on several measures that are keys to good health. When an individual is aware that his or her blood pressure or cholesterol are against the norm, he or she may take the appropriate actions to improve his or

her health. In today's environment, some employers are using these screenings in a more aggressive manner. The outcomes of these screenings are being used to drive the consumer's eligibility for a particular plan design, the level of cost share (e.g., deductible) within the benefit plan, and, in some cases, employment. Why the change?

"Employers have been employing wellness programs for some time, but are beginning to use these biometric standards as a means to get faster and more tangible results," reports Frank Crossland, vice president, MJ Insurance in Indianapolis, IN. Crossland views disease management and wellness programs as "identification tools that help keep healthy people healthy and improve the lifestyles of those with greater risk." Crossland is not alone. Some employers are using these indicators as a wake-up call for employees, not only in terms of understanding the impact on health, but also as a means to understand the impact of poor outcomes on their wallets. Learn more about the use of biometrics in Chapter 7.

The focus of wellness programs in the past has been on education and learning. Although consumers were educated about the need for exercise, the learning typically stopped there. Today, exercise, fitness, and physical activity programs are becoming commonplace in wellness programs. Using the workplace as a captive arena, organizations are focused on getting their consumers moving. Chapter 8 provides a detailed description of several physical activity initiatives.

Evaluate the benefit of a personal health record

Personal health records are emerging in the marketplace. Early forms of these tools were little more than a database held by the health plan in which the member could enter his or her health information. Some insurers populated the health record with pieces of data from processed claims, but this limited information offered far less than a full view of the consumer's

health. Information not provided by the health plan had to be populated by the individual, and this was a time-consuming process.

For example, many health plans do not receive member's lab results. The consumer would be required to obtain this information from his or her doctor and then manually enter the data in the health record. Those consumers who were diligent in entering and maintaining their information shared their personal record with healthcare professionals via paper. This approach is not exactly the high-technology process that many had envisioned.

These obstacles resulted in low adoption rates of personal health records. Consumers did not have the time to complete the information or simply weren't interested in doing it. In addition, individuals were leery as to what the health plan (or the employer) might do with the information. The concerns with personal health records mirror those of the health risk appraisal. Consumers worry that personal health information will be used to discriminate against them and deny them employment and/or health benefits. The lack of portability also made the health plan's health record less than desirable since many employers switch health plans every few years.

Progress is being made with personal health records, with several of the nation's top innovators developing prototypes. With advances in technology and emerging standards, personal health records should serve as a means to improve the efficiency of the healthcare system by sharing data, avoiding duplicate procedures, and preventing medical errors. An equally important outcome is the level of engagement that a personal health record may create. Having the consumer take ownership of his or her personal health record helps the consumer begin taking personal responsibility for his or her health. Jeremy Nobel, MD, an adjunct faculty member at the Harvard School of Public Health, also believes personal health records can help engage individuals in their health by providing personalized information. "Personal health records can guide individuals to appropriate services based on the individual's personal needs and circumstances. Education and information can be tailored to account for the individual's specific condition or health attitudes." Watch and evaluate the growth of personal health records. At this time, it's unclear who should sponsor (and pay for) this technology—the provider, employer, an independent third party, or the consumer.

Think beyond the employee

Workplace-based wellness programs have focused on employees, which is understandable since the employer sees these individuals for 40 or more hours per week. Health plans have gone beyond the employee and focused on individual member needs. Unhealthy dependents (adults or children) can significantly increase healthcare costs. A spouse may be a dependent on the employee's plan because he or she is unable to work due to a chronic illness. Dependents can have a significant impact on the bottom line. Equally as important, the spouse or significant other has tremendous influence and impact on your consumer. The partner may be the one driving the health of the household in one form or another. Whether it's deciding what to put in the cart at the grocery store to ensuring everyone gets to the doctor for preventive and routine services, our better halves have a great deal of influence on us. Individuals can't "go it alone." While they may have your support at work, they need that same amount, or more, of support when they're at home. This means we need to reach out and wrap the entire family in a Velcro hug! The following are some ways you can include dependents in your wellness programs.

Ways to include dependents in your programs

1. Offer dependents many of the services you offer to employees (as appropriate, of course). If the organization can afford it, offer these services to dependents for free or arrange for a subsidized or discounted price. It's just as important for the spouse as it is for the employee to know his or her

numbers and have access to clinical and wellness programs. Ensure that children are identified and enrolled in programs that can benefit them as well, such as those with juvenile diabetes or asthma. Figure out how to include kids in those wellness activities that may be appropriate. Provide childcare on the premises for the day of your health fair so the spouse can get access to the services he or she needs without having a toddler in tow.

2. If you're offering an incentive and rewards program, include the dependents. They'll be as motivated financially (and in some cases more so) than your employees. Determine whether rewarding dependents makes sense by understanding the disease prevalence for spouses and those under age 18. By using these age and family status indicators, you can begin to determine whether spouses and dependents are driving significant costs.

3. When sending educational materials to the home, address them to both adults in the household. Doing so sends the message that you want the spouses involved.

4. Create a family wellness newsletter with a separate pull-out section for kids. Use this section to help children learn about good diet, nutrition, and exercise habits. Give

them opportunities to earn rewards, like their own pedometer. Share examples of programs that are available to Mom and Dad at work so the kids can nudge their parents into activity or support them in a program. Showcase a child or a family that has worked together to improve their health. In some cases, health plans have started to offer games to engage kids in their health. This approach is certainly worth a look. The possibilities are endless in what you can do to engage all members of the family in your desire to create a culture of engagement around health. Just be sure to include the family members from the get-go to maximize your return on investment.

Customizing your wellness program....

Wellness programs are not "one-size-fits-all." Companies are customizing their wellness programs to fit the needs of their population. Critical to this customization are the ideas of bringing wellness directly to your consumers and creating a naming convention that helps drive a culture of health. The following are a few examples of companies that have tailored their wellness programs to meet the specific needs of their employees. These programs are designed to be targeted in nature rather than off-the-shelf. Customizing a wellness program ensures that funds are spent wisely on services that will have a positive impact on both the bottom line and the consumers.

 At Plexus Corp, in Neenah, WI a nurse is available to perform blood pressure and cholesterol screenings on a frequent basis. The company also offers physical therapy services in-house as a convenience to employees. A physician periodically leads "lunch-and-learn" sessions with employees on seasonal and other topics that are important to its employees. As an international corporation, Plexus extends its wellness to other countries. This includes placing a nurse on-site at its Mexico facility and assessing the ways to incorporate alternative medicine at its China location.

 Wellness programs are often privately labeled to create a connection to the company. "Well at Dell," the name of the health improvement and benefits program at internationally known Dell, Inc., is designed to create synergies with Dell's culture. "We have a culture of pay for performance," explains Clint Carlton, U.S. health and welfare program manager for Dell. "We also extend this same philosophy to our health improvement strategy." This program is both broad and deep in an effort to find something that will be attractive and engaging to every Dell employee. First and foremost, "Well at Dell" focuses on integration among all of Dell's

vendors, including wellness, pharmacy, and health plan partners. Employees in need of assistance can expect to receive one phone call from a single source, which allows for stream-lined, seamless processes. The Dell program also incorporates the use of incentives through health insurance premium reductions or contributions to a health reimbursement account. They also offer an on-site fitness center as well as quarterly fitness/wellness challenges to encourage employees to be physically active.

 The Montgomery County Hospital District offers a wellness program that energizes and motivates its employees. They began years ago by offering discounts on gym memberships, but the uptake was low. They incorporated a health risk appraisal into their program and identified key areas such as back injuries and weight management as areas to target first. They hired a chiropractor to shadow employees at work and get a firsthand view of how they were performing lifting tasks then created a course for employees to help them avoid back injuries.

The "Weight Watchers at Work" program provides half the payment up-front and the remainder when the employee has completed the program. The Weight Watchers program has been very successful, with 28 individuals losing 919 pounds in 33 weeks. "Success is breeding more success in our organization as a result of these programs," says Allen Johnson, chief administrative officer. The company believes that part of its success stems from the fact that the wellness programs are all employee-driven. At first, these programs were established by management and included employee participation on the committee. However, they have since turned the development and management of the wellness program over to a team of employees. These individuals are given broad parameters to work under but operate as a self-guided team.

 Cincinnati Eye Institute's "WOW" program (Working on Wellness) has its 400 employees engaged at all levels. The company's consumer population represents a diverse work force including patient service representatives, opthalmic technicians, billing personnel, and physicians. WOW provides an ongoing campaign of wellness initiatives to keep employees motivated year-round. WOW includes a pedometer program based on team competitions. They also introduce exercise programs late in winter to get individuals ready for spring activities. Weight Watchers and yoga classes have been added to the program as have blood pressure screenings and pulse checks. "WOW acts as a morale booster and stress reducer for employees," says Karen Maxwell, director of human resources. "We are trying to positively impact

behavior, but because the program is voluntary, it's fun for employees." The Cincinnati Eye Institute also takes its wellness initiatives one step further. Individuals can earn credits for participating on company committees and in volunteer activities. This expansion beyond physical health speaks to the need to embrace a holistic approach to wellness.

 Likewise, the School Board of Broward County, in FL, deploys a number of tactics in creating a robust program. From a "Healthy Heart" walking program (read more in Chapter 8) to the "blue line" (a quarter-mile marker that aids consumers in tracking the miles they have walked on campus) and Weight Watchers at Work, these programs are designed to address a variety of healthy lifestyle issues. "But more importantly, some of these issues speak to safety at work," states Ron Weintraub, benefits director. "The School Board of Broward County operates the second largest transportation system in the southeast United States. School bus drivers are required to ensure their blood pressure is within the appropriate range." To ensure that bus drivers "know their numbers," the organization has placed a blood pressure machine in the central transportation area for individuals to take their measurements regularly. If this program is successful, they plan to expand it to other facilities.

Providers and brokers can join the mix

Most wellness programs are driven through the employer since this structure provides the opportunity to gain access to all employees whether they are healthy or ill. Brokers and providers have an opportunity to assist employers in developing their wellness programs since they often have additional levels of expertise that may be lacking in the employer environment. Some brokers are serving as a general contractor or facilitator and pulling the various components of the wellness program together and offering them as a package to their clients. This approach is valuable to smaller employers who do not have the leverage to offer these programs on their own. The broker has a unique insight into the employer's needs and may be able to tailor a program while still maintaining a reasonable cost.

In other cases, brokers are looking to heath plans or third-party administrators to provide the services needed to support clients. "Brokers are interested in consulting with their clients but may not have the expertise or resources required to support a wellness or rewards program," states Karin Bultman, an independent consultant specializing in wellness and rewards programs. Brokers can often get support from their health plans through training and other collateral materials. In addition, some health plans will provide brokers with on-site wellness consultants to help evaluate client needs and recommend programs.

Many employers look to local healthcare providers to help them with health fairs, as well as biometric and other screenings. Today, employers have to reach out and attempt to locate the provider that's most appropriate and cost-effective for their needs. Providers should consider reaching out to employers and marketing their wellness services. They should offer a menu of services the employer can select from to meet their population and budget requirements.

In addition, healthcare providers that are at risk for medical expenses should ensure their consumers have full access to and are being made aware of the wellness opportunities available to them from the health plan. These providers must themselves be knowledgeable about what the health plan offers and must work in tandem with the health plan to get the message out to their population. When individuals seek care, the healthcare provider must seize this opportunity to engage them in these programs. When a consumer's healthcare provider talks with them about a particular program or service, it creates a powerful incentive for that individual to take the next action to learn about and enroll in the program.

The techniques and program approaches noted here are advantageous to both the consumer (convenience, access, and often cost savings) and the employer, who receives the productivity benefits and lower medical costs. If you're just now developing a wellness program or believe your existing program needs an overhaul, look at what some of these best-in-class employers have done and determine how you can make it your own.

The following are five simple steps to get you on your way to an effective wellness program:

1.   Review claims data in order to target issues that are relevant to (or emerging within) your consumer population.

2.   Carefully choose the programs you offer to maximize the return on investment.

3.   Create educational and effective communications to get your consumers engaged in and excited about your wellness program.

4.   Develop a private label that employees can easily relate to and one that will help drive the organization to a culture of health.

5.   Overcome budgetary constraints by looking to your broker, health plan, or local healthcare community to provide you with free or low-cost programs and services.

Remember, this is your wellness program. It needs to be relevant to your consumer population, and you are free to make it a wild success!

Refer to Figure A.8 in the Appendix for additional materials related to this chapter.

Rewarding experiences

Recommendations for creating effective, engagement-focused incentive programs

> *"The only way to keep your health is to eat what you don't want, drink what you don't like, and do what you'd rather not."*
>
> – Mark Twain

Adults know they should stop smoking, eat better, exercise more, and lose weight. And if the sales of goods and services in the diet, nutrition, and exercise industries are any indication, many are trying to do the right thing. Yet most consumers can't seem to get on the right track and stay there. Too many New Year's resolutions are broken, treadmills and other exercise equipment lie dormant in the basement, and reduced-calorie microwave dinners are supplemented with a handful of chips or a fattening dessert.

This failure to take control and improve health has not gone unnoticed, and the paradigm is shifting. No longer are healthy lifestyles—or lack thereof—a private matter. Employers are stepping into the fold and letting employees know if they want healthcare (and in some organizations, if they want to remain employed), they have to take steps to improve

their health. While individuals may grumble about this approach (some grumbling is in the form of lawsuits), most are accepting these changes as inevitable. Organizations are using a variety of tactics, including incentives and rewards, to get their consumers engaged in improving their health.

Incentives and rewards for behavior change

Incentives and rewards have been used over the years to encourage individuals to take a desired action, e.g., complete a health risk appraisal or stop smoking. Incentives and rewards have become much more prevalent in healthcare as employers desperately try to change behavior. The approach to incentives may include a "carrot," a "stick," or a combination. Organizations using the stick believe this is the only definitive approach to obtaining the employee's attention and gaining sustainable behavior change. Many organizations have implemented these approaches after years of trying the carrot. When softer attempts fail, they resort to more stringent tactics.

Incentives are actions the employer or health plan wants the individual to take, usually to improve his or her health. Some incentive programs focus on the individual engaging in healthy activity, which may or may not lead to ongoing behavior change, while others focus on healthy outcomes. Let's first explore the types of healthy behaviors that focus on engagement.

Activity-based rewards

Creating an incentive for consumers to take action toward improving their lifestyles is a very popular approach. Many organizations prefer this method because it sends a message to consumers that as long as they make a reasonable attempt to improve their lifestyles, the company will support them. The following is a look at some of the industry's more popular activity-based rewards.

Health risk appraisals
Chapter 6 described the health risk appraisal and how this method of data collection helps get a better picture of the individual's health status. Traditionally, employers have asked employees only to complete the appraisal, but

the current trend is to include spouses and even other adult dependents over the age of 18. The majority of organizations continue to make completion of the health risk appraisal optional. Many pay for completion through money back in a wellness account, the paycheck, or some form of health savings account.

These approaches have generated varying levels of success, with some organizations achieving higher participation than others. Common reward amounts vary from a low of $25 to a high of $100 for completion and usually serve to boost participation. Merchandise, days off, and other nonmonetary rewards have also been used. The success of the offering is dependent on whether the consumer believes the reward to be valuable enough to take the time to complete the appraisal. The challenge with offering a reward for completion of a health risk appraisal is that a definitive return on investment may be elusive. Employers and health plans hedge their bets that returns will come from increasing referrals to disease management programs or that completion will increase awareness of unhealthy habits and subsequently create the desire to change from unhealthy to healthy behaviors.

The landscape around health risk appraisals is shifting, with some companies requiring completion as a precursor to gaining health coverage. Using the health risk appraisal as a

 Engage! A Guide to Involving Your Consumers in Their Health

means to gain access to group health insurance coverage begins to change the way employees view their health benefits and chips away at the sense of entitlement that often accompanies these benefits. Organizations that have moved in this direction have typically tried the voluntary method, but understand that greater participation and positive outcomes are required to create the desired impact on healthcare costs. Communicate your decision, along with the rationale for requiring a health risk appraisal, to employees early to avoid surprises during the open-enrollment process.

Biometric screenings

Biometric screenings are often considered an extension of the health risk appraisal, and some organizations are rewarding the individual for simply participating in the screening. Creating consumer awareness about his or her personal statistics for blood pressure, body mass index, and weight may help create a desire for change. Remember, the very first step in engagement is to educate the consumer, and biometric screenings are a good way to start. Biometric screening outcomes are also used in other ways. Refer to the "Healthy outcomes" section, later in this chapter, for more details.

Biometric screenings are expensive, but the return can be good if the data is used. Before deciding whether to offer your consumers a biometric screening, understand how the data

will be put to use. Some vendors use the information in a one-time coaching session with the individual, while others incorporate it into a predictive modeling tool and use it to refer individuals to clinical programs. Lack of follow-through will send your consumers the wrong message and is a waste of financial resources.

Clinical programs

Clinical programs are incorporating incentives and rewards to encourage participation. Most health plans offer disease management programs as a means to help individuals with chronic illnesses better manage their conditions. Unfortunately, participation in these programs has not typically been high. Individuals may begin a program and then fail to complete it, or they may choose not to participate because they feel their condition is a private matter that does not require the involvement of the health plan or the employer. Signing up for a program alone does little to help the individual or to control costs. The key is ensuring that the participant is actively engaged every step of the way. Therefore, many programs are rewarding consumers based on completion of interim milestones and offering an even bigger payout upon completion of the program. The concept of rewarding small achievements helps motivate the participant to stay in the program and begin to make lifestyle changes. As with completion of a health risk appraisal, the amount of the reward varies and may be paid in the form of cash, credit, gift card, or contribution to a health savings or health reimbursement account.

Other wellness programs

Other similar approaches are being taken with regard to wellness programs, including nutrition, stress management, and back care. Health plans and employers are encouraging individuals to complete these educational programs by rewarding them for completion. Others also reward consumers for accessing a health coach on the phone or online, to help them better manage their health. Many health plans and employers believe that rewards are a very viable means of motivating employees and their dependents to take the necessary actions to change their behaviors.

Healthy outcomes

Positive changes in health status are needed to make a difference in healthcare claims cost. Engaging in healthy activities may or may not result in health status improvement. For example, exercising three times a week for at least 30 minutes is a healthy behavior. However, if the individual has a poor diet, smokes, and fails take his or her blood-pressure medication, the benefits of the exercise are not fully realized. Therefore, some health plans and employers are

taking the approach of rewarding consumers based on healthy outcomes.

One company that has designed a unique approach to outcome-based rewarding is BeniComp Advantage, Inc. Based in North Olmsted, OH, BeniComp Advantage provides supplemental group medical insurance coverage in conjunction with a high-deductible health plan (the employer can choose any health plan administrator) and a biometric screening. The employer typically chooses a plan with a deductible that is significantly higher than what it offers today. If the current deductible is $500, the new plan may have a $2000 to $2500 deductible.

BeniComp conducts on-site screenings for all employees and manages the employee communications. The screening is purely voluntary and an individual can choose to opt out of the program. For those that complete the screening, BeniComp looks at four key measures: blood pressure, LDL cholesterol, nicotine, and body mass index.

For every indicator that's in range, the employee can earn a credit ranging from $250-$500 apiece to lower the deductible. In the above scenario, if the deductible is set at $2500, the employee may earn up to four credits of up to

$500 each. Minimum and alternative reward programs are available to ensure compliance with the Final Rules for Nondiscrimination and Wellness Programs.

The health plan administers all set deductibles at $2500 and BeniComp tracks those employees that have earned credits. If an employee earns four credits, he or she has to satisfy a $500 deductible. Once the processed claims exceed $500, BeniComp begins to reimburse the employee cost share up to the amount of the credits earned. The health plan sends over claims information to BeniComp so the reimbursement is automatic.

In addition, BeniComp provides the employer a medical supplement policy that underwrites the risk for the amount of the credits that will be paid out to employees. The lower premium that the employer pays due to the higher deductible plus the premium paid to BeniComp is designed to result in immediate overall savings to the employer. BeniComp has also partnered with a few health insurers to create a combined offering.

One negative aspect of the program is that the employee does not have the opportunity to earn credits throughout the year. To overcome this problem, some organizations are providing two screenings—with one taking place several months in advance of open enrollment—to give individuals the opportunity to make improvements and qualify for credits. In addition, most employers offer this program in conjunction with a series of health and wellness programs that can help the employee improve his or her numbers and qualify for credits the following year. Organizations that implement the BeniComp program believe it's time employees take accountability for their health and that a program deeply linked to indicators that are known drivers of healthcare costs is an approach that will help engage consumers. BeniComp reports an average of 95% employee participation in the program.

 Virgin, the internationally recognized brand, has come to the United States to shake up the status quo and improve the health of individuals. HealthMiles from Virgin Life Care is a program that rewards individuals for physical activity as well as maintaining and improving health. The program consists of three key components:

1. The GoZone is a pedometer that records steps, and tracks miles walked and calories burned. The pedometer is also a USB device, which means the information it holds can be transferred quickly and automatically to the Virgin Life Care Web site.

2. The HealthZone is an easy-to-use touch-pad kiosk that captures weight, body mass index, body fat, and blood pressure readings. This kiosk is placed at the employer's worksite to provide easy access to employees. Individuals are asked to visit the HealthZone monthly to capture these key measures, which are then uploaded to the Virgin Life Care Web site where the individuals can track progress throughout the program.

3. The LifeZone is an interactive Web site that allows participants to log their exercise, view their key measures, and track the rewards they earn. Points can be redeemed for gift cards at a number of popular retailers.

HealthMiles is designed to get individuals active and motivate them to stay active for the long term. The ability to continuously earn rewards and participate in special contests known as challenges keeps participants coming back for more. Humana was an early adopter of the program and the first-year results have been impressive; participants lowered their blood pressure and improved their weight. Participation in the program has actually increased throughout the year, which demonstrates Virgin Life Care's ability to continue to motivate and engage participants.

Team-based rewards

Team-based rewards can be used as a means to increase program participation. For example, an employer may pay an individual employee $50 to complete a health risk appraisal and then pay an additional $50 if the percentage of employees completing the appraisal reaches 80%. Team-based approaches are also common for walking programs. Teams can be structured by the employer (based on a department, floor, plant location, etc.) or can be created by employees. The team that has the most steps will win a prize. These team-based approaches are designed to create camaraderie and encourage broader participation.

For the consumer, rewards come in different shapes and sizes, from debit or gift cards to wellness credits, contributions to a healthcare account, or receipt of merchandise. Each of these rewards serves to motivate individuals to take action. Because individuals are motivated differently, mix up your rewards offerings and determine which rewards give you the greatest return (or simply give your consumers a choice). If individuals feel they have a worthy goal to attain (beyond good health), they will work hard to achieve it. Many organizations have a limited budget and may believe that valuable rewards are out of reach. Read on to discover how even the smallest reward can capture a consumer's attention.

Some rewards programs operate on a "pay-as-you-go" basis, issuing the reward upon completion of each individual activity, while others operate on a points system. Under a points arrangement, the individual accumulates points and then turns them in for cash, equivalent debit or gift cards, or a piece of merchandise. Regardless of the method, different types of rewards can be offered.

Offer financial rewards

Financial rewards (cash or cash substitutes) are common. Debit cards, gift cards, and money back via the paycheck are appealing to the consumer and boost program participation. These types of financial rewards are easy for the consumer to understand and for the employer or health plan to administer. Most debit cards provide individuals unfettered access to use the funds on anything they desire (although these cards can be limited to healthcare provider locations only). Some health activists believe only rewards that reinforce healthy behaviors should be issued, while others prefer to give individuals the freedom to use the reward as they desire. Gift cards fall into the same category as debit cards. These cards may be limited to health-related merchants or used at a broader group of retailers. With the recent increases in gas prices, gas cards are a popular

option. If you decide to restrict the financial rewards to use at healthcare providers only, be sure to offer rewards that your consumers can use; otherwise, individuals may get discouraged and revert back to old behaviors.

Funnel rewards directly into a health account

Some employers want to tie rewards directly to further prudent use of healthcare services. These organizations prefer rewards in the form of contributions to a health reimbursement arrangement or a health savings account where the funds can be used only for qualified healthcare expenses. This reward approach is viewed as a way for the individual to build equity in the account; help buy down the deductible; and offset other healthcare expenses such as coinsurance, dental, or vision expenses. This approach also helps employees become more engaged in maintaining a healthy lifestyle as they begin to see money build in their account over time.

Use merchandise as a motivator

Merchandise continues to be used as a means to engage employees. At Plexus Corp, small rewards like company-branded coffee cups and T-shirts are successfully used as an enticement to increase attendance at "lunch-and-learn" sessions. Karen Maxwell, director of human resources for the Cincinnati Eye Institute, reveals that company-branded beach towels are one of the most highly requested rewards. Merchandise supports the "trophy mentality," which provides continuous reinforcement to the recipient as to how and why he or she earned the reward, further encouraging positive behavior.

Lower consumer cost share

Other forms of rewards focus on cost avoidance. Some examples include lowering or waiving copays or reducing employee premium contributions, a very common reward. Employees can lower their health plan premiums by undertaking any one of the wellness activities that have been discussed in this guide. One of the most common forms of premium reduction is tied to being tobacco-free or enrolled in a tobacco cessation program. One employer is using the premium reduction approach and tying it to outcomes from a biometric screening. They believe premium reductions to be an effective way to get employees to engage in healthier lifestyles.

Reward the community with your healthy initiatives

Offering a donation as a reward option encourages and enables individuals to transfer their rewards to a favorite charity or cause. Move beyond individual contributions and encourage your consumers to participate in community-based events that drive healthy

behaviors, such as walking or running events. Contribute to and match the donations your individual consumers earn independently and then donate these proceeds to the desired charity.

The employer, health plan, or provider's reward can be cost savings or cost avoidance, typically in the form of lower healthcare cost increases year after year. The organization might enjoy both types of financial rewards with reduced costs annually for a particular medical condition (e.g., diabetes) and lower healthcare trends in subsequent years.

Frequency of engagement

The challenge with many incentives and rewards programs is that they often fail to engage the individual over a long period of time. Many activities are short-term or singular in nature and fail to motivate true behavior change. Completing a health risk appraisal is an example of a healthy behavior that may or may not result in ongoing behavior change. The individual completes the appraisal and receives a reward; then what happens? To truly engage the individual, the output of that appraisal should be used to drive additional messages, activity, and incentives over the course of the plan year. If the individual's body mass index is too high, he or she should be given incentives over the course of the year to lose weight, by adopting a better diet and exercising more. If the individual has a family history of heart disease, he or she should be given incentives to adhere to his or her statin regimen. The ongoing nature of this contact is critical to engagement. A rewards program should be tied to periodic interactions with your consumers. Asking an individual to complete five activities in the first month of the plan year will probably not result in ongoing engagement in the rest of the year.

Conversely, allowing an employee to wait until the end of the plan year to complete the desired activities brings no benefit to the organization. Successful incentives and rewards programs keep the individual motivated year-round by either periodically introducing new activities or by regularly rewarding healthy outcomes.

Vary rewarded activities based on current behaviors

Rewards should be targeted and personalized and, with few exceptions, the employer should refrain from mass distribution of rewards. If rewards are given to individuals that are already engaged in the desired behaviors, you may be incurring expenses with little return. This is not to say that those who are doing the right things should never be rewarded. Rather, you may find your money better spent by rewarding

these individuals for different behaviors. A female who is currently compliant with all preventive services will not be changing her behavior based on a reward. Nor is she likely to stop getting these services if she is not rewarded and her peers are.

However, this individual may benefit from being nudged to the next level of engagement. She may respond to completion of a wellness program or participation in an exercise-based rewards program. Use limited rewards dollars wisely by ensuring that the rewarded activities are meaningful and will result in a positive change.

Program administration

An organization may choose to self-administer its rewards program if it's simple and straightforward. For example, providing gift cards or merchandise like T-shirts and coffee mugs for attending a "lunch-and-learn" session is better and less expensive for the employer. For a large-scale program, the organization may choose to outsource the administration. Year-long or points-based programs require detailed tracking of activities and earned rewards. Health plans may also be required to bill multiple employers for these programs. These more complex programs require a sophisticated rules engine that most employers, brokers, and health plans don't possess. Therefore, consider choosing a business partner that can handle the program administration more efficiently and cost-effectively.

Rewards programs are not set in stone; they are a work in progress. Some attempts will be successful and others less so. It will be important to set goals and measure your results to determine your successes and where improve-

ments are required. As with other engagement activities, expecting a return on investment in a single year may be wishful thinking. Rewards programs require long-term commitment and continuous modifications in order to maximize their success.

Refer to Figure A.1 and Figure A.2 in the Appendix for additional materials related to this chapter.

    Engage! A Guide to Involving Your Consumers in Their Health

CHAPTER  8

Get moving!

Strategies for incorporating physical activity
programs that motivate your consumers

> *"If it weren't for the fact that the TV set and the refrigerator*
> *are so far apart, some of us wouldn't get any exercise at all."*
>
> – Joey Adams, comedian/actor/writer

Today's lifestyles are hectic, with people constantly on the go. Parents are juggling full-time employment, chauffeuring their children from activity to activity, helping with homework, and managing the household. While consumers feel as if they are on the go more than ever, a sufficient level of physical movement is rare. The consumer sits in the car, at her desk, and with his or her child at the kitchen table. Without exercise, the typical consumer may only take 3,000 to 4,000 steps per day.

All of these responsibilities leave little time for exercise. Given a free moment, most adults would prefer to sit and relax rather than keep moving. As a result, people lead more sedentary lifestyles than they realize. Employers are beginning to understand the effects that leading a sedentary lifestyle have on medical costs, and they are taking action by introducing programs to encourage employees to step out

of their cubicles and get engaged in some form of physical activity. This chapter explores the tactics organizations are using to motivate their consumers to get moving.

On-site fitness centers

On-site fitness centers have been an early entrant on the wellness scene and have been embraced by employers, health plans, and some healthcare providers to encourage physical activity among their consumers. Fitness centers are popular because they're convenient and easily accessed by busy individuals.

The center typically accommodates early birds, the lunchtime crowd, and those who work out at the end of the day. If their work schedule permits, for example, employees can leave during the middle of the workday to take a spinning, Pilates, or aerobics class.

Subsidizing the cost of the fitness center is common to ensure individuals at all income levels have access. Organizations with multiple locations may provide discounts to other non-company-owned facilities if the cost of an on-site fitness center is prohibitive at each location. Most fitness centers have full-service capabilities, but may not provide the depth of equipment or the breadth of programs that a freestanding center provides. But the easy access and convenience more than offsets these minor deficiencies in most cases. Smaller employers may choose to band together to create a fitness center in a large office complex. Commercial real estate developers may look to create fitness centers for large, multiyear campuses. Some community hospitals have developed on-site fitness centers for their employees, as well as consumers from the surrounding community. The fitness center serves as an anchor in attracting individuals to the many services the hospital provides, ranging from traditional medical care to wellness and lifestyle improvement.

Special considerations

One challenge with the work-based fitness center is that some individuals will not use it due to self-consciousness. To a person that is out of shape, it seems that everyone in the fitness center is already in shape. The individual dreads appearing in an oversized T-shirt and old shorts next to some tiny coworker in a spandex outfit. You may not realize it, but

many of your consumers have this concern. Take the actions necessary to help your employees feel less self-conscious by allotting separate times or workout spaces for men and women. Separating the sexes may help put some individuals at ease.

To attract those individuals who are significantly overweight, hold a beginner's class customized to their needs. Traditional beginner's classes may be too much for larger individuals to handle. Help these consumers ease into a fitness routine at a level they can handle. Ensure that time exercising in chairs is a part of the workout and consider providing a private workout area for these beginners.

The same idea can apply to your older work force. Most individuals who are approaching retirement have no desire to keep up with a 20-year-old. They simply want to exercise to maintain good health. Make it easy for them to establish an exercise routine without feeling that they have to compete with a fit, 20-year-old coworker.

Opening doors to dependents

If a majority of your employees live near work, you might want to allow adult dependents access to the fitness center. Opening the center up to spouses will not only increase general use from non-employees, it might also encourage use by your employees who are nudged along

Engage! A Guide to Involving Your Consumers in Their Health

by their spouses. Consider sponsoring an evening or Saturday program as a means to educate younger children on activities they can do at home that will be beneficial. Offer a parent-teen night that invites older children to learn how to properly use the equipment. You may also sponsor racquetball or other tournaments with kids against parents or family against family. Including family members helps spread the message of health to your consumer's support system.

Train the trainers

Challenge your fitness instructors to think about what they can do to get those individuals that need more physical activity into the fitness center. Encourage them to explore what other employers are doing. Create an exchange program that allows your fitness instructors to travel to learn what other employers or well-recognized clinics are doing and then incorporate those techniques. Annual evaluations of your fitness center staff should move beyond the numbers of individuals using the center to the profile of the users. Success measurements should be based on the number of users that have made improvements in weight, body mass index, or blood pressure. Shifting the definition of success from the number of participants involved to actual improvements in health will engage your fitness center staff in your strategy to drive sustainable behavior change.

On-site fitness centers are not an option for all organizations, but this doesn't mean physical activity can't be encouraged. Employers are very resourceful, using the tools they have at hand to develop low-cost programs that meet the needs of their employees.

Other methods to get employees moving

The following are a few ideas that employers have deployed in an attempt to get employees out of their cubicles and into a more active lifestyle.

Support walking programs

The Virgin Life Care Health-Miles program, introduced in Chapter 7, is one approach to motivating and rewarding individuals. But organizations can create their own walking program by encouraging employees to put on a pair of tennis shoes and walk around the campus or the block. One company made a simple announcement on the intercom that employees could join together to walk at lunchtime and started a trend. A large number of employees joined the initiative and the only cost to this organization was a little bit of time and commitment. If funds are available, invest in creating trails that are well lit and safe for employees to walk on.

 The School Board of Broward County of FL hosts "Healthy Heart" walking contests. These challenges last six weeks and have departments compete against each other to see who can walk the most. Each participant is given a pedometer to measure his or her steps, and the team leader reports the results weekly to a wellness coordinator. The winners enjoy a healthy catered lunch as a prize. Using the retail concept of a secret shopper, this organization has gone one step (pun intended!) further than most. If an individual is "caught" taking the stairs or walking at lunch, he or she may be given a fresh bottle of water or a card that registers him or her in a drawing for a fruit basket.

For a less formal structure, suggest that meetings be held in different buildings so all employees have the chance to get some exercise. Unlock the doors in the stairwell to persuade employees to take the stairs rather than the elevator. If you have a large campus, post signs letting employees know how many miles (or steps) it is from one building to the next. The School Board of Broward County has a "blue line" on their campus that measures a quarter of a mile walked. The blue line helps employees gauge how far they have walked and serves as a subtle reminder to keep walking. Post signs in or near the elevators informing consumers of the steps they are losing by riding instead of walking.

Purchase or provide low-cost access to pedometers to help individuals track their steps. Continue to motivate your consumers to walk by providing a means for them to track their step activity. Set collective walking goals for your organization as a whole and publish how many miles your consumers have walked in total. Offer competitions for employees, departments, or self-selected teams to earn prizes. There is nothing more motivating than receiving a notice from your team captain that shows your team is slipping in the ranks. Healthcare providers can engage their consumers in these activities, as well. Imagine challenging your patients in the local community to track their physical activity. As discussed in the incentives and rewards chapter, help the community at the same time by sponsoring special walking events to support charity causes. Include the family members in this event and have a healthy refreshment booth at the end.

Encourage bike riding

Bike riding is becoming more popular as adults rediscover this joy from their childhood. The introduction of comfort bikes helps individuals understand they don't have to be Lance Armstrong to take a spin around the block. A half hour perusing the neighborhood or a short trip to work can reinvigorate the soul and help consumers become a little more active. How can employers help? Put bike racks in convenient locations for those who commute to work and include a sheltered area for protection against inclement weather. Organizations with large campuses may provide use of bikes for its employees to ride to other buildings for meetings. Walking trails can be used by bikers, so making an investment in these trails will gain the interest of both walking and biking enthusiasts. Older adults may be uncomfortable with the idea of a bike with hand brakes and gears. Offer a session to potential bikers letting them test different models. A local bike shop will sponsor the seminar and bring the bikes and the helmets as a means to promote their product. Ask them to sponsor a bike clinic for the kids on a Saturday morning to teach children about bike safety and maintenance. These types of initiatives cost the employer little more than some time locating a willing bike shop owner.

Think broadly about the concept of wheels. Include your rollerblade or skateboard enthusiasts in a broader "wheels" program. These sports are simply another set of wheels individuals can use to get some exercise. Provide facilities for individuals to shower and change clothes and a locker to store their skates, boards, and protective wear. Imagine how much fun it would be to see Mom and Dad rollerblading while Jimmy and Johnny are following behind on their bikes or skateboards. Expanding the

program concept from bikes to wheels opens up the opportunity for broader participation.

Promote sports leagues

In an era where it appears employees are willing to sue their employers over minor incidents, companies may be hesitant to encourage sponsored sporting events. Ask your lawyers to draft the necessary disclaimers, but don't shy away from these types of programs. They not only encourage physical activity, they also build employee morale. If your organization won't officially sponsor teams, allow your consumers to disseminate information and recruit individuals independently. Softball, volleyball, basketball, and golf are popular organized sports. Go bigger and broader by suggesting soccer, tennis, and field hockey. If your employees are mostly sedentary, start smaller with a ping-pong or pool club. While the physical activity is lower than desired, these types of programs meet individuals where they are and may be just the right level of exercise for an older population.

Create play zones on your campus that will entice consumers to step outside before, during, and after the workday. Build multi-purpose areas that can be used for a variety of activities to appeal to a broader base of employees. For example, a softball diamond can also be used for kickball and a volleyball court can be used for badminton or rollerblade hockey. As a small employer, talk with the other tenants of your building to determine the interest in creating a recreation area. After you have generated interest, collectively pitch your idea to the real estate developer or manager.

Bringing exercise to consumers

Building a fitness center or creating a play zone doesn't guarantee that all individuals will participate. We live in a "just-in-time" world and, as a result, many individuals are barely getting to their desks or workstations on time. Family and other commitments may keep them from coming in early enough or staying late enough to effectively use the fitness center. Here's a new twist—bring the fitness center to your employees. Ask your fitness center instructors to get creative and design workout programs that can be done at workstations or on the floor.

 Dell took this approach, offering a few minutes of yoga stretching exercises to its employees on the manufacturing floor. Employees get a few minutes of warm-up to start the day. Plexus Corp also has regularly scheduled exercise time for employees on the line or at a desk. These are smart ideas because they meet and engage employees where they are. It's hard for individuals to say they don't have the time when

exercise is brought to them as part of their routine workday.

Track the programs consumers participate in as a means to determine what programs are both popular and effective. Collecting this data at an individual level will allow you to determine which activities might be of greater interest by gender or age. This information can also be used to send targeted messages about new programs or to invite participation in focus groups. If you let consumers know how this information will be used, most will cooperate. If individuals are skittish about giving out this type of information, collect the data on an aggregate and de-identified basis as a means to keep your finger on the pulse of what interests your consumers.

Programs that encourage physical activity should be an integral part of any consumer engagement strategy. Why? Because these programs motivate people to get out, move around, and take some action. Avoid offering programs that appear to be extreme in nature. When the activity requires too high of a skill level, not only will the number of participants be limited, it may "turn off" individuals from participating in future activities. Remember to format your program like a good menu; mix up the types and levels of activities to ensure that your consumers will find at least one palatable activity.

 CHAPTER 9

What's for lunch?
Ways to promote healthy eating habits at work and at home

> "In general, mankind, since the improvement in cookery, eats twice as much as nature requires."
>
> – Benjamin Franklin

Food is a constant presence in our lives. We dine out with friends, take clients to dinner, and create elaborate spreads for holiday and family celebrations. Often, we eat at our desk and in front of the television. Our waists have grown in direct proportion to the size of the cup holders in our cars.

Food permeates the workplace as well. With on-site cafeterias, vending machines, working lunches and birthday celebrations, food is a part of our daily work routine. It's hard to create a culture of health when food—and unhealthy food at that—appears at every turn. A healthy culture can't exist without healthy options.

Let's examine the ways food impacts your work force's health and approaches to ensuring that you offer healthy alternatives at every turn.

Examine the cafeteria

Organizations that are fortunate enough to have a cafeteria should work with their cafeteria partner to ensure they understand the organization's desire to create a culture of health. Fresh fruits and vegetables should be available and affordable to employees. If a salad costs significantly more than a cheeseburger, those on a budget will opt for the cheeseburger. Work with your cafeteria manager to create cost-shifting to the less healthy options and subsidize healthier fare. Ask your partner to eliminate trans fats and ensure they cook with healthy oils and nonstick sprays.

Healthy eating goes beyond fruits and vegetables. Offer low-calorie and high-fiber breads—not all multi-grain breads are as healthy as they look—and offer light spreads as toppings. Use fat-free and low-fat milk, sell light yogurt and light cheese, and offer baked potato chips. Eating healthy does not mean deprivation. Sweets can be offered with light alternatives for those who choose to indulge while watching their weight. Bring employees into the fold by having them submit healthy recipes that your chefs can test in the cafeteria. If you offer a program such as Weight Watchers at Work, try incorporating some of their products into the mix. Use the cafeteria resources to offer a healthy cooking class to your consumers (don't forget to invite the spouses). Help your partner focus on portion control. Too much food (even healthy food) will work against your goals.

Consider being more direct in connecting eating habits to your employees' health. Place a scale or a blood pressure machine near the cafeteria. Perhaps reinforcing the connections between eating habits and health will help individuals to think a bit more carefully when choosing between the hamburger and the chicken.

Many organizations don't have an on-site cafeteria. However, your employees probably eat the majority of their lunches at a few local restaurants. Talk with these restaurant owners about creating healthy options for dining in or taking out. Create a mechanism for employees to place their healthy orders online and have them delivered to your workplace. (No cheeseburgers allowed!) If you're a small employer, join with other companies to make changes.

Tackle the munchies too

Vending machines should not be overlooked in your quest to improve health. The companies that stock these snack machines will tell you healthy snacks don't sell when sitting side-by-side with unhealthy snacks. Be diligent. Work with the vendor to determine what healthy snacks are available. Peruse the Internet in search of alternatives if you're not provided with satisfactory answers. Consider fresh snacks that may appeal to your employees, e.g., veggies and dip or sliced fruit.

Drinks shouldn't be overlooked. What's the ratio of bottled water to sodas? If the soda is significantly outnumbering the water, cut back on the soda. Ask the snack vendor to introduce flavored waters as an alternative to some of the soda selections. Also, offer caffeine-free alternatives in the vending machines. Once again, charge more for the unhealthy snacks (including the liquids), to subsidize the costs of the healthy snacks. At one manufacturing location, the plant manager removed the snack machines altogether in an effort to improve the health of his employees. Swap out the snack machines altogether for healthy snacks that you provide for free to employees. With this approach, you control the offering. Not sure what to do? Ask your employees for their input. They'll be creative and will be more likely to buy in to the ultimate solution.

 Think beyond the snack machines and get creative. At Highmark Blue Cross Blue Shield, Anna Silberman, vice president, preventive health services, took it upon herself to create a farmer's market in the plaza outside the corporate headquarters during the summer. Employees spent their lunch hours selecting fruits and vegetables for their snacks and to take home to their families. She has since started the "Good Apples" program, which delivers fresh fruit and produce from Pittsburgh's famous strip district to the company cafeteria for easy pickup by employees.

Send the right message at business meetings and celebrations

It's important to walk the walk when you're trying to drive a culture of health. Business meetings often involve food, whether it is muffins for breakfast or sandwiches for lunch. It's time to review your office menus and perhaps the catering service. Whether it is breakfast, lunch, or dinner, you can control the menu. Even fast-food restaurants are offering healthier fare, e.g., baked potato chips and fruit as a side dish.

Celebrations of individual and company successes are a way to motivate employees. Recognition of personal events such as birthdays, marriages, or births helps bring the team closer together. Delicious cakes are the standard fare because they're inexpensive and serve a large number of employees. One company still serves cake as part of its celebrations but has switched to angel food cake with fruit toppings. In organizations where individuals take turn bringing in the snacks, suggest that they bring in light options and share their recipes with the other team members. Holiday celebrations are also a good opportunity to encourage your consumers to create delicious dishes that don't stretch the waistband.

 We've examined approaches for healthier food alternatives at work, but what can we do when the employee leaves the office or the plant? In truth, there's only so much you can do, but education will go a long way. If you continue to keep healthy eating at the front of their minds, everyone will find at least one healthy option to be of value. The Cincinnati Eye Institute used a taste test as a means to encourage healthy eating. A nutrition table was set up in the lunch room where employees sampled food that included low-calorie and low-fat substitutes. "The idea was to show employees that eating healthy can be simple and delicious."

Karen Maxwell states. Letting individuals experience these alternatives firsthand encourages them to incorporate healthy foods into their diets.

If a doctor was asked to predict a patient's future health status sight unseen with no medical history, could she do it? Probably not very well, but what if she were able to peek at the individual's grocery cart? This may be a reasonable proxy for predicting one's future health.

A cart full of eggs, bacon, white bread, and cookies might be indicative of an existing or future problem (e.g., obesity, high cholesterol, etc.). While a cart full of leafy green vegetables and fresh fruit is not a guarantee of health, at least it's a start. While we can't extend our reach to the grocery store and monitor what people put into their carts, we do need to consider the impact of these purchases on consumers.

Many consumers are not fully aware of nutritional guidelines and have little idea how to shop for healthy foods. For some, fruit

consists of sticky roll-ups or powdered strawberry drinks. It's been a very long time since most consumers have had a lesson in nutrition, and most could use a refresher. A robust wellness platform might include teaching consumers to read nutrition labels and understand the subtle nuances that may lull them into buying unhealthy options. Helping consumers make better choices when they shop is another way to embrace them in the Velcro hug.

Individuals that have participated in group-based diet programs know that a key benefit of these interactions is that people share information with each other. This type of collaboration can be effective at the workplace as well. Encourage individuals to share healthy foods they've discovered, including details on where the goods can be purchased. Create a Wiki, a billboard (electronic or otherwise), or have a whiteboard available in a common area where employees can post this information. If participation is low, create some excitement by offering prizes or rewards for the best recipe or tip of the week.

CHAPTER 10

Is there a doctor in the house?

Approaches that foster consumer-physician partnerships

> *"I regret to this day that I never went to college.*
> *I feel I should have been a doctor."*
>
> – Ty Cobb, baseball hall of famer

The role of the healthcare provider is changing from an all-knowing, take-charge professional to that of a healthcare advisor and guide. Of course, there are still many individuals who prefer their doctors to remain in the driver's seat; it's easier that way. The patient simply goes along for the ride, taking the prescriptions, getting the necessary exams, and remaining totally and unabashedly unengaged.

For many consumers, however, access to information through the Internet, television, books, and health magazines have forever changed their view of healthcare professionals. These consumers view healthcare providers as professionals who will provide them with advice and help them navigate through the healthcare system. This role implies that consumers are at the helm, steering the ship, and that the ultimate decision and responsibility for health lies with the consumer and not with the doctor.

This chapter includes ways to encourage consumers to engage in a dialogue and be a partner in health with their healthcare provider. In this chapter, we discuss the need for a personal physician and explore some programs and tactics healthcare providers are using to remain competitive in an ever-changing environment.

Help consumers identify a personal physician

While consumers are more apt to take charge, the shift away from HMOs and some cities' increasingly limited access to family physicians has resulted in a valuable piece of the healthcare equation, the primary care physician, being lost. In the early 1990s, consumers displayed their opposition to restrictive rules around access to specialists, diagnostic procedures, and hospital services. In the process of rejecting what was perceived to be a barrier to care, the baby may have been thrown out with the bathwater. The shift to point-of-service and preferred-provider-organization plans, meant, in many cases, that the health plan member was no longer required to select a primary care physician. The option to identify a primary care physician then faded from the enrollment form and the medical identification card, leaving many individuals wondering whom they should turn to for care. "We lost a key positive connection between the primary care physician and the member over the possible hassle of a referral, limiting our option of specialist care," explains Ken Olson, president, Horton Benefits Solutions. "Every member should have a personal physician tracking all medical care and consulting the member on options available to maintain and improve health."

This is not to suggest that an individual be required to select a personal physician, but it is important to help consumers understand the importance of establishing a relationship with a doctor who will know them and their medical history and help them navigate the healthcare system. A personal physician may include a cardiologist or an OB/GYN and does not need to follow the traditional definition of primary care physician. Some health plans are exploring the concept of a medical home and paying certain providers for service in a coordinator

role. While this is an admirable approach that certainly warrants additional investigation, you can simply start educating consumers on the importance of having a personal physician and then provide them with a means to identify and engage with one.

Consumers may also need assistance in finding a physician that meets their needs. Perhaps a family member has special needs, the family is new to the area, or the individual simply doesn't know what to look for in selecting a physician. Employers, brokers, health plans, and providers alike can help by providing consumers with a checklist of items to aid them in their decision-making. Encourage individuals to schedule an interview with the physician and get a tour of the office. Encourage them to check things like whether the staff is helpful and whether the doctor's credentials are readily displayed. The surest sign that a physician or practice may not be a fit is if they refuse an interview.

Whether you are providing questions or a physician checklist, make this information readily available to your employees. Keep it on your organization's Web site, in the break room, or in the cafeteria. Send information home so the spouse, who may be the healthcare decision-maker and care coordinator, can have access as well.

Help your consumers prepare for doctor visits

The relationship an individual has with his or her doctor can make a big difference in health. Those who feel comfortable having a dialogue with their physicians will more likely be compliant with their treatment regimen because they participated in and agreed with the plan of action. However, many individuals don't feel comfortable having a conversation with their doctor. This discomfort stems from many sources, including the reverence many have for their doctor to the more common reason that there is limited time available to talk with the physician.

Assume that the typical doctor/patient visit is 15 minutes. With this limited amount of time, the doctor has to examine the patient, ask pertinent questions to ascertain history, diagnose the problem, and then explain the issue to the individual. These activities may leave little time for the patient to ask the questions needed to gain a better understanding of the situation. Help consumers by preparing them before they visit the doctor.

Encourage your consumers to write down a description of their symptoms and to note when and how often they occur. Having this information at hand will help the doctor in assessing the situation. In addition, suggest that consumers write down questions beforehand and take notes during the office visit. These simple practices will aid the individual in remembering pertinent information.

During a focus group examining how confident its associates were in using its consumer driven plans, Humana discovered that some of its associates were uncomfortable with and unsure of what questions to ask the doctor. The company addressed this issue by creating a wallet-sized laminated card with routine questions to ask during a visit. The questions are simple and easy to understand. They are useful not only for associates, but also for students who are away from home and may be seeking healthcare services without the benefit of having Mom or Dad around. The following are sample questions to provide consumers:

- Why are you recommending this treatment?

- Are there other alternatives that I can consider?

- What will this prescription do for me?

- How often do I have to take it and how?

- Is this a generic medication?

♦ Are there any side effects that I should watch for?

Healthcare providers take note. Consider making your practice or hospital more efficient by providing consumers with the information needed to encourage a dialogue. Many providers currently offer information about a particular treatment or service. They assume the consumer will read this information and understand everything he or she needs to know. Sometimes, the consumer may fear that asking a question might upset the doctor or a hospital staff member. Let your consumers know that not only do they have a right to have a dialogue with their physicians, they need to have the dialogue. The dialogue will ensure they understand the agreed-upon treatment plan and what is expected of them to actively participate in the process.

Explore consumer- and convenience-based services

In the last two decades, mergers and acquisitions resulted in large healthcare systems that dominated a particular region. Smaller, less capitalized or less efficient hospitals were closed or absorbed into the new behemoths. Employers and health plans alike struggled to get meaningful discounts for services because there were little to no options in the market. More recently, hospitals have been in a building mode, expanding capacity and services.

However, the healthcare market is changing. Recent advances in technology have resulted in a shift of many procedures away from the hospital and into freestanding ambulatory settings. New market entrants are performing services that were traditionally performed only in a doctor's office. This market shift has created a competitive environment and, subsequently, opportunities for entrepreneurs to fill in some existing voids to increase access and convenience for consumers.

Concierge medicine

One example of a new healthcare model designed with the consumer in mind is the concierge practice. Also referred to as "boutique" medicine, these practices significantly reduce the number of patients in the practice in order to focus on and spend more time with the patient. Access to these practices comes with a price, as the consumer is required to pay a fee simply to become a member of the practice.

Typically, the fee covers the initial comprehensive visit, provides access to the doctor 24/7, and may include the doctor making home and emergency room visits when necessary. The doctor continues to bill the health insurer for routine office visits and services. Still, some providers refuse to deal with the health insurance company at all and charge the consumer a much higher fee. The individual then recovers payment from the health insurer directly.

The advantage of these practices is that the doctor has significantly more time to spend with the individual. This allows the doctor to focus on creating a preventive care plan and help better manage those with chronic conditions. Advocates of these practices say that more hands-on management by physicians will lead to better care for the consumer and perhaps result in better utilization. Should consumers be encouraged to use these practices? If you believe that these practices have value, consider reimbursing all or part of the fee as part of your wellness program. You may also consider reimbursing the fee for those individuals with chronic conditions that enroll in a disease management plan. Although there is little published evidence as to whether these practices have an advantage over traditional medical practice, it makes sense that more hands-on management by a qualified health professional can only help those with chronic conditions better manage their care.

On-site clinics

Over 50 years ago, some employers introduced the idea of on-site clinics to provide medical care to employees. Some of these clinics turned into group practices and others became health maintenance organizations. What's old is new again, with the reintroduction of medical clinics on-site at major employer campuses. The clinics range from providing minor care only to facilities staffed with physicians and routine diagnostic capabilities to provide primary-care services.

Convenient care clinics

Employers are embracing on-site convenient care or "quick" clinics to improve employees' access to care and provide additional convenience. While the average office visit may only last 15 to 20 minutes, individuals are often kept waiting in overcrowded doctor's offices, resulting in lost work time. These sites are not designed to treat major or chronic conditions, but they provide a valuable service for individuals who need attention for minor illnesses such as sore throats, pink eye, and earaches. Individuals may turn to these clinics when they can't get access to their personal physician. These clinics may also serve as an alternative to the emergency room.

Critics claim that these clinics may increase unnecessary utilization of healthcare, while advocates believe this access gets patients medical attention early when illness can be more readily addressed. Early studies show that most consumers use these convenient care clinics appropriately and still maintain a relationship with their personal doctor. In addition, consumers have been highly satisfied with the services they have received. This is a model that doctors need to watch. These clinics may skim off minor services, leaving the personal doctor with a schedule full of intense

cases, which may or may not be more con-
ducive to the way a personal doctor prefers
to practice.

On-site primary care clinics

 Employers are also investigating
the provision of more comprehen-
sive services to employees
through the creation of on-site primary-care
clinics. Frank Crossland, vice president, MJ
Insurance, Inc., in Indianapolis, is helping to
lead a collaborative effort among several of his
large clients to develop primary-care centers
with physician and diagnostic services. The
approach is unique in that it provides services
for employees and their dependents and includes a fitness center as a key component.
Employees can complete a health risk appraisal
through kiosks, share the information with
their doctor, and participate in on-site disease
management programs. The center will be
designed to encourage employees to obtain
preventive and routine services and will include
access to low-cost medications that will manage
short-term and long-term conditions.

Crossland states, "Although there is a financial
investment in the development of a primary
care center, we know that if we can get people
to change their lifestyles and comply with
appropriate treatment options we can reduce
unnecessary medical and drug utilization
overall and reduce costs."

As with the on-site clinic described above,
hospitals and other healthcare providers are
partnering with nontraditional entities to bring
healthcare to the masses. In April 2007,
Wal-Mart issued a press release stating that it
planned on opening as many as 400 in-store
clinics by partnering with local hospitals and
other organizations. Why are hospitals engaging in these unique partnerships? Healthcare providers want to retain the existing
relationships they have in their local communities and, as such, are willing to try new
business models.

Not all employers can afford to have on-site
clinics, but they can help employees by providing lists of local minor-care clinics, low-cost
urgent care centers, and primary care
physicians accepting new patients.

Community partnerships

Many healthcare providers are working hand-
in-hand with governments, employers, schools,
and other institutions to improve health in
their local communities. These initiatives are
designed to create awareness around issues
that are specific to the local community. These
partnerships may occur in large communities
or in small rural areas. They may be well-
funded or managed on a shoestring budget.

Whatever the situation, these partnerships
serve to improve the health of the community

and may be an avenue for you as an employer to tackle healthy behaviors.

 The Community Health Partnership (CHP) in Harrison County, KY, brought together industry, government, and education to create programs to address this community's most pressing health issues. Since cardiovascular disease is a leading cause of death and disability in Harrison County, CHP initiated programs throughout the community, beginning with the school system, to emphasize the importance of nutrition and exercise. They focused on improving county residents' cholesterol measures and cardiovascular health through "Go Red" initiatives for women's heart health. In this rural area, they worked together to get a full-time cardiologist in the region. "What may seem like simple initiatives make a major difference in a rural community," states Stephanie Barnett, a consultant for the Community Health Partnership. Barnett assists in the development and implementation of these programs. Employers should talk with their local healthcare providers and gain an understanding of the providers community's needs. By partnering with these, you may be able to help not only your employees but your community.

 Another example of a small community hospital with big ideas and the will to implement them is the Windber Medical Center located amidst the coal mines of western Pennsylvania. Windber Medical Center is mostly recognized for its recovery efforts for Flight 93, the plane that crashed near the small town on 9/11, and the rescue of the Quecreek miners. This hospital has proved to be formidable not only in rescue efforts, but in efforts to improve the health of its community.

President and CEO Nick Jacobs, one of the first hospital administrators to write a blog, has pushed the envelope to make Windber a place where individuals can get healthy and lead fulfilling and well-balanced lives. Jacobs knows firsthand that lifestyle can lead to illness and that a positive change can lead to health. Diagnosed with heart disease, Jacobs embraced the Dean Ornish program as a means to reverse his cardiovascular disease. He saw the dramatic improvement in his own health and felt so strongly about the program that he made it available to members of his community through the hospital. But he didn't stop there. Jacobs has created a holistic approach to health, offering classes ranging from nutrition to spiritual healing and pet therapy. The hospital operates a state-of-the-art on-site fitness center available to anyone 14 years of age or older. "Windber takes a holistic view of health. We understand that the emotional aspects of health are as important as the physical aspects and we want to provide our patients with all the support they need," says Jacobs. Windber has created a health destination that not only heals the sick, but also helps keep people healthy and active."

 Duke University Health System offers its consumers Web access to schedule appointments and pay balances, and they will soon be providing them with access to a personal health record. "If you provide individuals with access to their health record, you empower them to be their own health advocate," says Monte Brown, MD and vice president for administration. As with other health systems, Duke also invites individuals from the community to participate in advocacy and safety committees. These individuals provide the organization with feedback and input on new facilities, programs, and services.

Employers or health plans may wonder why it's important that healthcare providers take these steps to engage consumers in facility and

program design. It's simple: You're footing the majority of the healthcare bill so you'll want to be sure that the providers are doing everything they can to create a safe and effective environment for your consumers.

In addition to engaging consumers in their health, providers play a dual role, both rendering healthcare services and providing health coverage to their employees. In fact, many hospitals are often the largest employer in a particular region. This means that they, like other organizations, struggle with rising healthcare costs. They also understand the impact on productivity when employees call in sick. They use a variety of programs and services to engage employees in their health and promote wellness.

At the end of the day, healthcare providers have a full view of the impact of an employee's health on the overall system, and most providers are taking the necessary steps to engage their employers and consumers in healthier lifestyles.

CHAPTER 11

Getting the support you need

Six engagement-boosting services
your health plan may offer—if you ask

> *"In the long run, we shape our lives, and we shape ourselves.*
> *The process never ends until we die. And the choices we make*
> *are ultimately our own responsibility."*
>
> – Eleanor Roosevelt

Whether you believe it is the employer's role to drive healthy behaviors, or it is the employee's responsibility to step them up, your health plan can help you design and implement a program that's right for your employees. Many, but not all, of the activities described in this guide are available from a health plan. Some of the unique activities, such as exercising at your desk or conducting a low-fat taste test, won't likely be within the scope of the health plan's offering. Regardless, you can look to your health plan to at least provide a baseline offering to get you started. Let's do a quick review of the services you should expect from your administrator.

Data analysis

Organizations (employers, providers, and brokers) that have a sufficient number of employees can usually receive an analysis of claims data for their population, along with a summary of the potential areas for improvement. Based on this analysis, the programs and services that will have the most benefit in the short- and long-term for the consumers as well as the organization should be chosen. Small employers may not be able to get a detailed breakout; however, the health plan can still make some recommendations for areas on which to focus based on the employer's type of industry and geographic location. For example, a manufacturer located in a region notorious for allergies and whose employees do a lot of heavy lifting might want to focus on back care and allergies to start. Claims experience should be reviewed with the broker and health plan representative every three to six months to stay on top of emerging trends and issues.

After engagement strategies have been implemented, the health plan can also be a source of data analysis to determine the impact of these initiatives. Brokers and consultants also provide these services. Claims should be reviewed on a year-by-year basis with a focus on the problem areas to determine where improvements have been made and whether the engagement tactics have had a positive effect. One area where most health plans are deficient (because they don't typically have access to this data) is in reporting the effects of these engagement strategies on work productivity. A health plan may be able to provide this analysis if the employer provides the data; otherwise, the broker or consultant can assist. Pulling in productivity data helps organizations get a true picture of the financial return these engagement strategies can generate.

Clinical programs

All major health plans provide a broad range of case-, disease-, and demand-management programs. Using claims data, they can tell the employer or brokers the number of individuals (employees and dependents) that should be enrolled in the health plan's clinical programs. Many employers are tempted to carve out these programs to save on cost, because they prefer a particular feature that the health plan does not provide, or because the vendor is touting a greater ROI. A key to disease management is the integration of data. Without data, oppor-

tunities for referrals into clinical programs may be missed. When considering a carve-out of these programs, be sure that all the data is getting to your vendor in a timely manner, and make sure your vendor is doing something with the data. Without the appropriate data exchange, the program will not be fully effective.

Employers that self-fund their medical plan should know that these clinical programs may require an additional charge. Fees are typically based on the number of program participants or spread across all employees. The fees should be calculated both ways to determine which fee arrangement makes better financial sense.

Also, employers will need to determine whether the health plan or vendor is willing to guarantee a return on investment. While many provide this guarantee, there is a wide variation in the data analysis and, at times, the business case is built on a broader book of business and not exclusively on an employer's population. Disease management and other clinical programs provide a valuable service to individuals with chronic conditions. If there were not significant value in these programs, health plans and other vendors wouldn't be offering them. Whether or not a significant return exists on these programs, they help consumers better manage their conditions. Providing this support to consumers is the right thing to do.

Engage! A Guide to Involving Your Consumers in Their Health

Wellness program components

Health plans offer a good foundation for a wellness program; however, these programs typically lack the high customization that has been shared in this guide. Choosing to use the health plan's programs depends on several issues. First and foremost is cost. Basic wellness services, such as online content and self-serve programs, are usually offered by the health plan free of charge. Online and telephonic coaching services and rewards programs likely require an additional fee. The health plan may also offer a wellness consultant who can evaluate current program offerings and make recommendations for improvement. These individuals can also help an employer develop and coordinate the implementation of a wellness program. Consultant services require an additional fee but are a good way for smaller employers that lack resources to provide a comprehensive program to their employees.

Gain an understanding of the programs available from the health plan and the corresponding cost. Save those limited wellness dollars for another customized initiative when the health plan offers basic services for free. As discussed earlier, health plans integrate data from their various wellness programs, such as the health risk assessment, into its clinical models to drive program participation. When considering who to purchase a wellness program from, look at the entire picture, from enrollment to data exchange and costs, and factor in the value of integration.

Education

One of the most time-consuming initiatives is educating and communicating with your employees. As discussed earlier, effective programs continue on a year-round basis and consist of various forms of contact. Health plans can provide a comprehensive education program based on the types of benefit plan designs offered. Based on the employer's size, the health plan may be willing to provide on-site open-enrollment support and ongoing "lunch-and-learn" sessions. Brokers also provide these services.

The content provided by the health plan should include topics from fitness and wellness to the myriad of conditions or illnesses consumers may face. This information is disseminated periodically throughout the plan year and often ties into national campaigns such as breast cancer awareness. Some employers choose to develop their own content, often citing the fact that they offer multiple health plans and want to ensure consistency for their employees. While this approach is commendable, many health plans have conducted research and employed highly skilled professionals to create these materials. Take full advantage of the expertise the health plan offers, and focus your attention and internal resources on the custom needs of your population.

Decision-support tools

Health plans have spent a great deal of time and effort building or purchasing tools to help individuals choose or use their benefits. These tools help individuals:

+ Choose the most appropriate benefit plan

+ Find lower-cost drug alternatives

+ Share the average cost of an office visit

+ Determine the amount of money the individual should contribute to a health savings account

These tools are critical in getting consumers to change their behavior, so most organizations will want to take full advantage of what their health plan has to offer.

Decision-support tools are typically available free of charge, and the health plan will provide educational sessions to encourage people to become familiar with these tools. Some health plans may also be able to provide a report on the number of individuals using the tools.

Equipped with this information, the employer or broker can determine whether additional educational support is needed to drive adoption of these tools. For organizations whose consumers have limited access to computers, work with the health plan to bring in additional equipment during the open-enrollment period. Even when consumers have access to the Internet at home, they often like the feedback of their coworkers during open enrollment; providing the additional support will help these individuals become more engaged in the enrollment process.

'Lessons learned' data

Many health plans offer their products and services to their own employees first. This "test and learn" concept offers the health plan the opportunity to get feedback from highly engaged individuals (your employees will always be the first to tell you what they didn't like!) and then make the necessary changes before rolling the plan out to the broader marketplace. When considering offering a particular program, ask your health plan representative whether its employees and others were part of a pilot. Have them share with you the lessons learned so you can avoid the same potential pitfalls. Have the health plan provide a step-by-step implementation to ensure a smooth and timely rollout.

Ready, set, engage
An overview of your new engagement plan

> *"Before anything else, preparation is the key to success."*
>
> – Alexander Graham Bell

Throughout this guide we've reviewed a variety of tactics and approaches that employers, brokers, consultants, and providers have taken to engage consumers in their health. We've explored what to do and how, where, and when to do it. But how do you pull it all together? How do you create a cohesive strategy and plan to create sustainable engagement and behavior change? "The concept of consumer engagement is still developing," states Kim Bellard, vice president of eMarketing and CRM for Highmark Blue Cross Blue Shield. "Success depends not just on the health plan, but also on the employer and how they push it. If the employer doesn't have a clear strategy then they won't see the desired results."

Embarking on your journey

While creating engaged consumers is not a simple process, it's not impossible. Organizations with limited resources can effectively create a culture of health; the process may simply take a bit longer. Regardless of the amount of resources available, every organization should have a plan for success. This chapter outlines the basic steps we've discussed that employers need to follow to embark on their journey toward improved consumer engagement.

Envision a culture of health

Envision a culture of health, including what success will look like in your organization, and write it down. The vision of health has to be tailored to the organization. While it's helpful to look at what other organizations have done to engage their employees, each organization is different. The vision must be aligned with an organization's own philosophies and culture. Documenting a vision of the future will help others in the organization gain an understanding of where the company is. Having this

---

common understanding will help get key individuals on board with the transformation. In addition, a written version of the vision will serve as a benchmark to assess whether the programs and tactics are in sync with the desired outcome. The vision should have some goals in it, although at this stage, specific numbers may not be known. Creating a vision statement does not have to be an elongated or overwhelming task. Simply think of the issues of importance to your organization that should be effectively addressed when creating a culture of health. The following are a few key items that may be considered when drafting a vision statement:

+ Employee morale

+ Productivity

+ Employee/consumer awareness of healthcare costs and impacts of their actions

+ Employee/consumer/client retention

+ Controlled healthcare costs

+ Commitment from management and the rest of the organization.

The following is an example of a vision statement:

A vision of health for ABC Company
The impact of health on ABC Company and its associates is readily understood by all, from the senior management team to the associates in the field. We will create an awareness of health with our associates through ongoing communication, education, and transparency. We will reach out to and engage associates and their dependents to improve their understanding of health and the impact of lifestyles and behaviors on their own health as well as on our business. We will try new, unique approaches to educating and engaging our associates and will infuse the topic of health throughout all channels of communication. We will measure our efforts and modify programs, services, and tactics as needed to improve. Driving to a culture of health is a journey. We are committed to the long-term health of our associates and ABC Company's bottom line.

Get commitment

Obtain the necessary buy-in from senior executives to move forward with your plan. Make an assessment as to how much information you need to provide the senior team up-front. If you believe your management team might be a bit leery of changing the organization's culture, scale back on your plans. Begin by offering some small, incremental changes or approaches to get the okay to move forward. Remember that a ringing endorsement is not always needed. As long as the management team is not objecting to the plans, consider this as permission to move forward. Be prepared to provide information on the funds needed to begin the journey. Information concerning return on investment may also be needed. Develop the level of detail that you know your senior team will want. If they want to get into the weeds, let them; if they only need a topline view, then limit the information accordingly.

Determine the level of employee involvement (and perhaps involvement of consumers in general). Will your organization have an employee governance or steering council, or will employee involvement be limited to an advisory capacity? Some sort of employee involvement in the development process is highly recommended. Determine a method for soliciting employees for their assistance. A formal council will require strong consideration of the participant attributes.

Focus efforts on high-impact areas

Gather the data and conduct the analysis as to what programs and services will have the greatest impact. When conducting the analysis,

go beyond the claims data. Look at your productivity information and your physical plant. Assess the cafeteria, vending machines, and food menus, focusing on how you will incrementally make changes to improve eating habits. Don't forget about undertaking efforts such as preventive services that will help keep healthy people healthy. Include dependents in the mix to maximize the impacts of engagement. Work with your health plan or third-party administrator to determine the services it offers and the corresponding costs. Unless the programs are poorly structured, take full advantage of the free services offered. Minimize unnecessary expenses to maximize return. If other vendors are required, conduct a thorough assessment of their capabilities and costs. Look to local healthcare providers who might be willing to provide on-site services at lower costs (or for free).

Establish specific goals

Now that you've identified the major areas of focus, determine the goals for success. These goals may take the form of participation in clinical or wellness programs, reduction or stabilization in claims costs for a specific condition, or use of online tools and information. Ensure that the data can be collected to effectively measure the goals. Determine where your organization stands today in relation to your goals. This will ensure that the new objectives are fair and truly represent an improvement. Ask for industry standards to determine how your organization compares today. Be realistic in determining the number of activities to be measured. Creating too many goals up-front may result in a loss of focus. Report your progress on a quarterly basis. Using a reasonable time frame allows you to adjust your tactics if you're not seeing the desired results.

Create the education plan

Develop a year-long plan for educating and communicating with your consumers. Include a representation of the communications individuals may be receiving from other areas of the organization to avoid communication overload. Determine how you will infuse the topic of health into every touch point with your consumers, including written communications and meetings. Reiterate the idea that good health permeates everything you do. Look to the health plan or broker for communications materials and content to avoid expending resources unnecessarily. Pace the rollout of the various initiatives so as not to inundate consumers with so many choices that they give up and take no action.

Motivate your consumers

Develop a strategy to motivate your consumers. Will the use of incentives and rewards be an integral part of your strategy? If so, think this approach through. Will you offer a long-term

points-based rewards program, or will smaller rewards be issued based on completion of desired activities? Assess your internal capabilities for administering a rewards program and, if needed, engage outside vendors to handle this aspect of your program.

In order to really walk the walk, work with your internal health activists and consumer engagement champions. Help create a plan for these key individuals to educate and motivate your consumers. The plan can include ideas on how to raise and discuss the issue of health at meetings and in one-on-one discussions, as well as how to factor it into department budget planning. Talk with these individuals about what they have done or are doing to improve their health; encourage them to share their stories and progress with employees. This personal touch by leaders within the organization will help individuals relate and will provide them with some additional motivation to tackle their own unhealthy behaviors.

Measure your progress and provide feedback

Faithfully measure the progress you are making. Be consistent in your methodologies to ensure that improvements are valid. Provide the information in a way that your management team and consumers can understand, tailoring the message to each audience as appropriate.

     Engage! A Guide to Involving Your Consumers in Their Health

Consumer involvement from inception is critical. Having consumer input in program design helps ensure that you will meet the needs of your population. However, a broader group of consumers should be engaged in providing ongoing feedback to ensure your engagement tactics are working. Include tactics such as focus groups, in-depth interviews, and surveys in the overall plan. Remember that feedback works both ways. Be sure to include a timeline for communicating with management and employees on your efforts. Let them know what has and has not been successful. Provide them with advance notice of changes that will be coming so they can be prepared if the changes impact them personally. Providing feedback keeps you true to your promise of transparency and helps consumers feel that their input really can make a difference.

Make changes at a pace your organization will tolerate

Assess the level of tolerance of your organization for change and then push the envelope just a bit. Lay out the initiatives, draw the line at the level of change you think your organization can handle, and then take it one step further. This will become your change target for the year. This approach forces you to give your organization some credit in the level of activity they can handle; it is always more than we think. This tactic also helps to avoid making changes that are so broad that they cause backlash.

The desire to create a culture of health may drive us to make significant changes too quickly. Consumers often react negatively to the smallest change; if the changes are too dramatic, you may face significant backlash. You can move swiftly and push the envelope without wreaking havoc. As your consumers become more educated and the issue of health becomes ingrained in your culture, you can and should step up the pace, becoming a bit bolder each year. The level and pace should be well thought out and should be an integral part of your overall plan.

Conclusion

An effective engagement strategy will require you to serve as the lead architect. This guide was designed to be used as a reference tool. In it you found various approaches and tactics used to engage consumers in their health and create sustainable behavior change. You've most likely found some ideas you like and others that would never work in your organization.

Consider these ideas as a place to start or an option that deserves a closer look. Select those ideas that resonate and use them as building blocks to be part of a greater structure. Use other resources and talk with peers in other organizations to determine what has driven their successes or caused their failures. Develop your strategy and incorporate evolution, as things will most certainly change over time. Engaging consumers in their health is a journey that will take time and patience.

It's my hope that this guide has served to reinforce to those that have been trying to create culture of health that they are on the right track and that success looks different in every organization. For those of you who are just getting started, know that you can drive change in your organization or with your clients. Create a plan, lay a foundation, and begin making changes. Your organization will not only adapt, it will thrive, and your consumers will benefit from your ability to wrap them in a Velcro hug.

Appendix

FIGURE (A.1)

Low-Fat, Low-Calorie Dessert

Bake-off

Monday, September 25

Entries must be prepared by an HMH employee or a family member living in the employee's household. To qualify as a low-fat, low-calorie dessert, entries must have 5 or less grams of fat and 300 or less calories per serving. Include recipe on entry forms located at the time clocks. Submit dessert and entry form to the Executive Dining Room by 11:30 a.m. Monday, September 25. Four judges will score entries by appearance (20 points), texture (20 points) and flavor (60 points). All participants receive 5 fitness bucks and 5 frequent mover miles. The employee submitting the winning dessert receives a basket of kitchen items valued at $50.

Source: Courtesy of Community Partnership, LLC. Reprinted with permission.

FIGURE (A.2)

HealthTrip Rules

1 Earn frequent mover miles and cash them in for rewards and chances in drawings. Mileage is earned when you do aerobic, recreational, or physical movement activities.

2 Use the HealthTrip exercise log to track your mileage each month. Just write your frequent mover miles in the square below the date on your log. Turn in your log at the Ticket Booth outside the cafeteria during the first week of each month. If you can't stop by when the Ticket Booth is open, see Mollie Smith (marketing).

3 Earn miles by participating in other HealthTrip educational and physical events. Watch for a list of events and their mileage values each month. You'll receive a HealthTrip Ticket after participating in each event. Log the miles you earned in the square under that date in the "Challenge and Events" section of your log. Turn in your HealthTrip Ticket with your log at the end of the month.

4 Earn at least 50 frequent mover miles each month to receive 20 fitness bucks and become eligible for the monthly prize drawing.

5 Get at least 50 frequent mover miles in January, February, and March to receive a free pair of socks from John's Run/Walk Shop.

6 Win a trip to Gatlinburg! Employees who earn at least 50 frequent mover miles in 6 of the 10 HealthTrip months and participate in at least one other employee fitness program are eligible for the grand prize—a two-night stay at a Gatlinburg motel, dinner for two at Applewood Farmhouse Restaurant, and a $100 gas card. Other employee fitness programs include:

Jazzercise ....attend at least 10 classes per month for 3 months
Wellness center.........visit at least 10 times per month for 3 months
Smoking cessation.....remain smoke-free for 6 months after completing smoking cessation classes or quitting on your own
Weight loss ....lose 10% of your initial body weight and maintain the weight loss for 6 months
5K walk/run ....complete the Born to Run or another 5K walk/run

7 Get information on the next month's city/site at the Ticket Booth outside the cafeteria during the last week of each month. If you can't stop by when the Ticket Booth is open, see Mollie Smith (marketing).

8 Register for HealthTrip at any time during the trip. Just stop by the Ticket Booth outside the cafeteria during the first or last week of each month or see Mollie Smith (marketing).

FIGURE (A.2)

How to Earn Frequent Mover Miles

Please refer to this conversion chart as you log your frequent mover miles.

AEROBIC EXERCISE – Any activity that uses large muscle groups, can be maintained continuously, and is rhythmic in nature. Examples of aerobic exercise include:

    fitness walking
    jogging/running
    cycling
    cross-country skiing—outdoors or on indoor equipment
    aerobic exercise classes
    swimming
    stair climbing

Aerobic exercise time converts into frequent mover miles (FMMs) according to this formula:

    1 FMM = 20 minutes of aerobic exercise
    1 FMM = each additional 10 minutes of aerobic exercise

Example: A participant walks 40 minutes and earns 3 frequent mover miles

    Time = First 20 minutes + 10 minutes + 10 minutes = 40 minutes
    Miles =   1   +   1   +   1   = 3 FMMs

RECREATIONAL ACTIVITIES – Includes activities such as volleyball leagues, basketball leagues, golf leagues, racquetball, tennis, and other sports.

Recreational activity converts into frequent mover miles (FMMs) according to this formula:

    1 FMM = One hour of recreational activity
    1 FMM = Each additional 15 minutes of recreational activity

Example: A participant played golf for 1.5 hours and earns 3 frequent mover miles.

    Time = First hour + 15 minutes + 15 minutes = 90 minutes/1.5 hours
    Miles =   1   +   1   +   1   = 3 FMMs

PHYSICAL MOVEMENT MILES – Shorter periods of frequent movement during the day. These miles are based upon the new fitness guidelines which indicate that even short, periodic episodes of physical movement can improve one's health. The goal is to encourage and reward participants for making modest increases to their overall activity level each day. Movement miles would include any 10-minute physical movement period during the day in activities like these:

©2007 HCPro, Inc.   **Engage! A Guide to Involving Your Consumers in Their Health**

FIGURE

vacuuming
housecleaning
raking leaves
taking the stairs
going for a walk during a break
parking the car farther from the mall or store and walking

Physical movement converts into frequent mover miles when participants accumulate several shorter periods of physical movement during the day according to this formula:

1 FMM   = 3 physical movement periods which last for **at least 10 minutes each** during one day
0.5 FMM = each additional 10-minute physical movement session

For example: A participant vacuumed the house before leaving for work, walked 10 minutes over the lunch break, took the stairs from the first floor to the tenth floor for a meeting, and walked around the block with her children in the evening.

Time =   vacuuming +   walk   +   stairs   + evening walk
          (10 minutes) (10 minutes) (10 minutes) = 30 minutes   (13 minutes)
Miles =   1 FMM for cumulative 30 minutes + .5 FMM for additional 10 minutes = 1.5 FMM

HEALTHTRIP CHALLENGES AND EVENTS – The handout for each month's city/site will include simple word finds, quizzes, crossword puzzles, and fill-in-the-blank activities. Each HealthTrip challenge you complete and turn in with your log converts into 5 frequent mover miles. Educational and physical events will be scheduled each month for you to earn extra miles. For example, attend a Lunch-N-Learn or watch it on video to earn 5 frequent mover miles. Or join in planned activities—like jumping jacks in the maintenance hallway during lunch—to earn another 5 miles.

If you have questions about HealthTrip, contact one of your HealthTrip Travel Coordinators:

Sandy Avery	3546	Mary Sue Grubb	3511
Crystal Baker	4351	Margaret McGuffin	3530
Diane Burton	3524	Cathy Muntz	3505
Patrick Carroll	4167	Marlene Riggle	3560
Ricky Cordray	3534	Mollie Smith	3510
Chuck Duffy	3502	Ellen Whitaker	3520
Rhonda Gaunce	3522		

FITNESS/HealthTrip-Rules
11-29-05/cjm

Source: Courtesy of Community Health Partnership, LLC. Reprinted with permission.

FIGURE

How to Prepare for a Medical Procedure

If you find out that you are in need of a medical procedure, the following steps may ease the process.

♦ Log onto the **www.humana.com** website or call Humana at 1-800-626-2694 to check that your medical provider is still participating with the ChoiceCare Network before each visit.

♦ During your visit ask for an explanation on what will happen, how the procedure will be coded and who will be involved during the procedure (specialists, anesthesiologist, assistant surgeons, etc.).

♦ If your procedure requires hospitalization, your medical provider must contact your insurance carrier for pre-admission review and notification. To check if your provider has completed this process, contact the Humana Customer Service Department at 1-800-626-2694.

♦ If you have questions contact **Concert Health Resources** (1-800-275-8744) or **Humana** (1-800-626-2694).

Source: Courtesy of Sarah Novak of Plexus. Reprinted with permission.

FIGURE **A.4**

Get the facts about your medications

Next time your doctor offers you a prescription, ask these questions. The answers to them can help you use the medication safely.

1 How will this drug help me?

Ask your doctor what your prescription is specifically for.

2 Is a generic available?

If you doctor has prescribed a brand-name drug, ask about a generic alternative medication. Generics can save you up to 80% on the cost of the drug.

3 How long should I stay on this medication?

It's important to find out how many days you should take the medication and how to take it, what to do if you miss a dose and how many doses are needed before the next refill.

4 Is there anything I shouldn't take while I'm on this medication?

Ask your doctor what foods, drinks, over-the-counter medicines, other prescriptions or activities I should stay away from.

5 What side effects can I expect?

Not everyone experiences side effects but it's best to be prepared and ask your doctor about common side effects and how to deal with them.

Remember to check out Humana's Pharmacy Tools on your *MyHumana* web page for a variety of additional resources.

Source: Courtesy of Sarah Novak of Plexus. Reprinted with permission.

FIGURE **A.5**

HMH Wants to Help
You and Your Family Members
Give Up Tobacco Products

- Employees can purchase prescription Chantix for $20 per month. Some people give up tobacco products in one month using Chantix; others require up to three months. Obtain a prescription from your physician and take it to Cathy Muntz in Administration.
- HMH will supply employees' first package of nicotine-replacement patches, gum or lozenges free of charge…whether they take tobacco cessation classes or quit on their own. And employees can purchase additional patches, gum or lozenges at greatly reduced prices—about half the retail price.
- Any family member or public person can purchase reduced-price nicotine-replacement patches, gum or lozenges if they attend tobacco cessation classes at HMH. This is offered as part of HMH's mission to improve community health.
- Each employee can also purchase reduced-price gum, lozenges or patches for one family member living in his or her household who does not participate in tobacco cessation classes.

One-month prescription of Chantix..$20
Two-week supply of 21 mg nicotine patches............................24
Two-week supply of 14 mg nicotine patches............................24
One-week supply of 7 mg nicotine patches..............................14
48 pieces of 4 mg nicotine gum..6
50 pieces of 2 mg nicotine gum..9
48 pieces of 4 mg lozenges...27
72 pieces of 4 mg lozenges...32

Email Cathy Muntz to order supplies. Allow 1 to 2 working days for delivery. Supplies will be distributed at tobacco-cessation classes or can be picked up from Cathy.

- Employees who give up tobacco products receive 500 fitness bucks or a $50 gift card to the store/restaurant of their choice when they have been tobacco-free for 3 months and another 500 bucks or $50 card 6 months later.
- Employees who have been rewarded for tobacco cessation in the past will receive 1,000 bucks or a $100 gift card when they have been tobacco-free for 9 months.
- To be eligible for bucks or gift cards, employees must measure their CO level by breathing into Respiratory Therapy's "smokerlyzer" weekly during the first 3 months and monthly during the next 6 months. Just stop by Room 156 on first floor.

Fitness/Smoking/Product Prices-070919
9-19-07/cjm

Source: Courtesy of Community Health Partnership, LLC. Reprinted with permission.

Engage! A Guide to Involving Your Consumers in Their Health

FIGURE

Realize Your Benefits ...   Today's Benefits Buzz
Volume II, Issue 5

Transparency Overview

In the world of health care, <u>transparency</u> means having access to data (hospital performance ratings, cost comparisons and more) that can assist you in making informed decisions.

This tool estimates the average provider cost for a particular procedure.

Costs can vary substantially from provider to provider, and, although your share of costs may be minimal, depending upon your benefit plan, the level of costs could eventually affect your deductible or coinsurance, and future health insurance on its cost-sharing fees.

Please utilize this helpful tool to compare costs between hospitals and providers for certain inpatient and outpatient procedures.

Do not avoid getting health care based on the cost information. Medical decision-making should be done in consultation with your physician. Use this information to talk with your physician.

The transparency tool can be found on PRIDE > HR Website > Benefits > Health > Transparency Comparison Tool

At Plexus, we realize more than products, we realize possibilities.

REALIZE YOUR FUTURE

Source: Courtesy of Sarah Novak of Plexus. Reprinted with permission.

FIGURE  A.7

CURRENT EVENTS DEVELOPED BY THE CHP WELLNESS COMMITTEE	
Event	**Date event was developed**
Little Feet, Big Feet Family Fun Walk/Run	**September 11, 2002–Present** Held annually in collaboration with the Born to Run/Taste of Harrison County. Participation continues to rise.
Little Feet, Big Feet Healthy Sundae Party and School Competition	**2004–Present** Party for the classroom with the most participants in the walk. Class also receives a basket of school supplies valued at over $100. School with the most participation is awarded the traveling plaque. All elementary schools compete yearly for this award.
HC Schools "Children's Health Fairs"	**February 2005–Present** (Held health fair and then encouraged each school to take over. 2 schools continue to have health fairs. CHP participates annually in all.)
Longest Day of Play	**June 21, 2006–Present** Longest day of the year (summer solstice). 300+ in attendance for our first event. Huge success; will continue annually.

LISTING OF EVENTS THE CHP WELLNESS COMMITTEE CURRENTLY PARTICIPATES IN OR HAS PARTICIPATED IN SINCE ITS DEVELOPMENT IN 1999. (The list below reflects the CHP Wellness Committee's direct participation as a committee or as individuals.)	
Community Health Fair	**2000-Present**
Go Red for Women	**2004-Present**
Get Fit Kentucky (fitky) (Several committee members are a part of this "internet" group. FitKy keeps up to date on Kentucky's meetings, outlooks and grant availability. Its main focus is childhood obesity in KY.)	**2004-Present**
HC Schools Children's Health Fairs	**2005-Present**
Harrison County Fair	**July 2004 - Present**
Kentucky Obesity Steering Planning Committee	**March 2004, 2005**
Great American Smoke Out	**November 2002, 2003, 2004, 2005**

EVENT DEVELOPED BY THE CHP WELLNESS COMMITTEE THAT ARE NO LONGER IN PROGRESS.	
World Run Day (campaign for research for ALS/Lou Gehrig's disease)	**November 2000, 2001** (Committee opted to end the participation to focus more on different events)
"Don't Eat Your Heart Out" Healthy Heart Food Fair	**February 2001** (Event held at the High School. Great turn-out. Opted in 2002 not to due again due to lack of community interest)
"Harrison Healthy Harvest"	**July 2001** (Weather hurt event. Decided time of year not good for committee to commit to because of vacations, etc..)

Engage! A Guide to Involving Your Consumers in Their Health

FIGURE **A.7**

CHP Wellness Committee Goals & Focus
1999–Present

1999: Initial purpose/goal of the CHP Wellness Committee

The committee was developed in 1999 as a subcommittee to the CHP Employee Advisory Committee (EAC). The official name is CHP Employee Advisory Wellness Subcommittee. The committee's role was to coordinate the implementation of the community-wide health initiatives that would create measurable impact on improving the health of the community. The main focus was improving cardiovascular health in the community.

2002 Goals

Committee focused on 3 health initiatives: Nutrition, exercise & smoking cessation. Committee would focus on established events within the community and attach on to them to promote goals and awareness. The committee established their first child-focused event; Little Feet, Big Feet Family Fun Walk. The fun walk would be an annual event established by CHP Wellness.

2003 Goals

Committee added goals to be reviewed yearly in addition to the already set focuses previously mentioned:

- Become more aware of availability of grants and conduct planning to apply for these grants.

- Improve and broaden our efforts in the Community Health Fair.

- Repeat the "Little Feet, Big Feet" event

FIGURE (A.7)

- Find an advocate for school age nutrition

- Recruit 2 new members (District Food Manager, student from HOSA (vocational healthcare class) attend meetings)

- Continue with previously set goals of promoting heart disease awareness, good nutrition, exercise and smoking cessation through continued education.

2004 Goals

The committee began to steer towards school-age children and their greatest health risk; childhood obesity. Childhood obesity was incorporated into the initial focus.

2005 Goal

The committee decided to continue their steer towards younger children with the main goal changing to strictly **CHILDHOOD OBESITY.** The committee will work with school-age children promoting prevention methods and will incorporate smoking cessation, heart disease awareness, physical activity and nutrition into **CHILDHOOD OBESITY,** the main plan of focus.

2006 to Present

The committee's main goal will continue to be **CHILDHOOD OBESITY.** The committee will focus on the following established events: *Children's health fairs within all elementary schools, continued committee membership to the Go Red for Women campaign of Harrison County, Community Health Fair, Longest Day of Play and Little Feet, Big Feet Family Fun Walk (Sundae party and school competition).* The committee will continue to be a strong advocate within the community and does not look to change the main focus of **CHILDHOOD OBESITY** in the future.

Source: Courtesy of Community Health Partnership, LLC. Reprinted with permission.